Menorca Tour & Trail Map

tunning clarity

assively detailed

enerous 1:40,000 sc

dispensable for wal

dventurers

quipped for both GPS and/or compass
avigation

ght up to date

est map you can buy - at any price

Ask

r s

We

rca maps
nce your
n more.
good
or direct
ublishers.

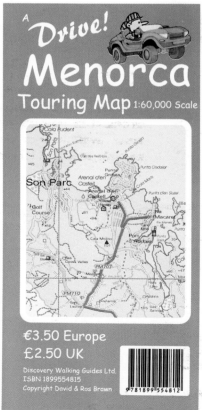

A *Drive!*

Menorca

Touring Map 1:60,000 Scale

Son Parc

€3.50 Europe
£2.50 UK

Discovery Walking Guides Ltd.
ISBN 1899554815
Copyright David & Ros Brawn

ass

Ther

The map sections used in this book have been reproduced and adapted from **Menorca Tour & Trail 1:40,000 Scale Map** ISBN 1-899554-86-6, second edition, and from **A Drive! Menorca Touring Map** ISBN 1-899554-81-5 (partial street plans used in the Maó and Ciutadella town walks). Both maps are published by **Discovery Walking Guides Ltd.** 10 Tennyson Close, Northampton NN5 7HJ, England.

"Tour & Trail" Legend

ROADS, TRACKS & TRAILS

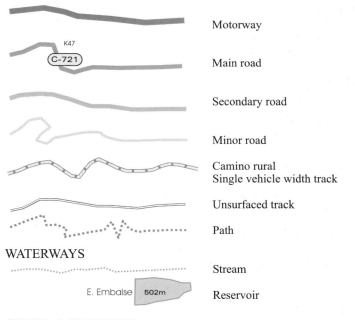

Motorway

K47
C-721   Main road

Secondary road

Minor road

Camino rural
Single vehicle width track

Unsurfaced track

Path

WATERWAYS

Stream

E. Embalse   502m   Reservoir

GENERAL FEATURES

🕯 Lighthouse	≼ Mirador, viewpoint	⬤ Spring
⌂ Tower	ℹ Information	⛽ Petrol
⚱ Ermita, chapel	⌂ Hotel	⎚ Bar/Restaurant
⊡ Football, sports ground	⊼ Picnic area	⊓ Historic Site
⛪ Church	⊞ Cemetery	⊕ GPS Waypoint

🐢 Sightings of wild tortoises

All our country walks include GPS Waypoints. These refer to specific points along each walking route. In order to use these GPS Waypoints (which are also grid references on the **Menorca Tour & Trail Map**, ISBN 1-899554-86-6 pub. Discovery Walking Guides Ltd.), remember to set your GPS datum to **European 1950**. Using the wrong datum can result in significant errors in location.

Menorca lies within the area of **39°48.000** to **40°06.000 north** and **3°47.000** to **4°19.000 east**. When inputting the Waypoints into your GPS, do remember to include the degrees; e.g. the roundabout at Cala Galdana, 56.480N 57.633E, should be input as 39 degrees 56.480 north and 3 degrees 57.633 east.

Do remember that GPS Waypoints are approximate, and while we quote positions to 0.001 minutes of arc (approximately 1 metre accuracy), in practice 0.010 minutes of arc (approximately 10 metres accuracy) is an acceptable standard of accuracy.

Waypoints alone are no substitute for a written walk description, but will ensure that you are heading in approximately the right direction. Additional waypoints as a further aid to navigation may be plotted from the Menorca Tour & Trail Map.

For traditional 'Map & Compass' navigators, the GPS Waypoints also act as exact map grid references for the Menorca Tour & Trail Map. Within the walk descriptions, general compass directions are given (e.g. NW is north-west) to ensure that you are heading in the correct direction.

Two walks have no GPS Waypoints; the Maó and Ciutadella town walks. The narrow streets and tall buildings mean that your GPS cannot 'see' sufficient satellites to obtain a reliable location fix.

Please note that on the Menorca Tour & Trail Map and on the sections from it which are reproduced in this book, the symbol for each GPS Waypoint is placed alongside the walking route for clarity, not on the exact location to which it refers.

- our rating for effort/exertion
1 very easy   **2** easy
3 average   **4** energetic

- approximate time to complete the walk

- approximate walking distance in kms

- approximate ascents/descents in metres

- from **0** (none available), up to **5**

(exceptionalfood/drink/position)

There are more prehistoric remains concentrated into the island of Menorca than anywhere else on earth, and there are likely to be more still lying undisturbed under fields and undergrowth. Even those that have been excavated or at least cleared of bushes and earth can easily be visited at no charge. Some of the more important and accessible sites have information boards and car parking areas, while others feel untouched by recent centuries. Some are easily reached by road, while others can be accessed only on foot.

There is also plenty of history from less distant eras. Menorca's coastline boasts many watchtowers, dating from the 16th to the 19th centuries, and the remains of other military establishments, also dating from the 16th century and up until the Spanish Civil War. The cities of Maó and Ciutadella and many of the other towns are all steeped in history.

Most walks on Menorca will have some historical interest; in fact, it is difficult to avoid. For those particularly interested in walks with historical content, try these:

Walk 3	**Torre d'en Penyat**	Defence tower dating from Napoleonic times
	Castell de Sant Felipe	18th century Fortress
Walk 7	**Trepucó** Settlement	Menorca's biggest *taula*, a majestic *talaiot,* a *hypostyle* chamber
Walk 12	**Trebalúger**	Large *talaiot* within a walled enclosure
Walk 14	**Torrelló**	A *talaiot*, and a sixth century mosaic church floor, Fornas de Torrelló
Walk 15	**Talatí de Dalt**	Prehistoric settlement
	Rafal Rubí Vell	Two *navetas*
Walk 18	Unnamed settlement	Prehistoric *poblat* and *naveta*
	Torre de Sa Nitja	Watchtower
Walk 19	**Cap de Cavalleria**	Gun emplacements
Walk 20	**Mola de Fornells**	Abandoned barracks
Walk 23	**Torre Blanca**	Prehistoric *poblat*
Walk 25	**Torre d'en Gaumés**	Large prehistoric settlement, including *talaiots*, *taulas*, *hypostyle* buildings and a water storage and filtration system carved from the rock
	Lluc al Lari	Military camp
Walk 27	**Son Bou Basilica**	Remains of early Christian Romanesque church
Walk 29	**Santa Agueda**	Site of Roman castle, with additional fortification added by the Moors
Walk 32	**Talaia d'Artrutx**	Watchtower
Walk 33	**Es Tudons**	Prehistoric *naveta*

(A brief explanation of words in italics can be found in the glossary on page 77.)

Much of Menorca's countryside is characterised by gently rolling hills and dales, green meadows and thickets of trees. Many fields are divided by pale stone walls which provide habitats for many varieties of plants and insects. The wilder areas of the island include wetlands, rugged cliffs and a coastline blessed with bays and beaches. The clean air and lack of pollution, along with the lack of major developments and industry, ensure that plants and wildlife thrive.

Trees, shrubs and plants

Common trees that you will see on a number of our walks include:

olive (*Olea europea*)   **holm oak** (*Quercus ilex*)
strawberry tree (*Arbutus unedo*)   **Aleppo pine** (*Pinus halepensis*)
mastic tree (*Pistacia lenticus*)

There are many shrubs and plants commonly found on our walks, including:

tree heather (*erica arborea*)   **myrtle** (*Myrtus communis*)
gladioli (*Gladiolus communis*)   **French lavender** (*Lavandula stoechas*)
rock rose (*cistus* - various species) **sarsparilla** (*smilax aspera*)
wild rose (*Rosa sempervirens*)   **Italian sainfoin** (*Hedysarum coronarium*)

Also look out for members of the **lily family**, **asphodels** and **orchids**, as well as a wide variety of more humble wild flowers and grasses.

Birds

Menorca is home to many species of resident birds, and also plays host to migrating and over wintering varieties. You will usually see some bird life in all areas of Menorca, but areas of particular interest to bird watchers are:

       S'Albufera of Es Grau (Walk 24)   Aveagua (Walk 21)
       Galdana Gorge (Walk 30)   Son Bou (Walk 27)

Just a few of the commonly seen birds:

Cory's Shearwater	**Mediterranean Shag**	**Egyptian Vulture**
Booted Eagle	**Stone Curlew**	**Rock Dove**
Scops Owl	**Hoopoe**	**Tekla Lark**
Fan-tailed Warbler	**Raven**	**Sardinian Warbler**

Wildlife

You will see **lizards** sunbathing on rocks or hear them scuttling into the undergrowth. There are three varieties on Menorca;
Lilford's wall lizard with a distinctive rather stubby tail shaped something like a turnip, the **Moroccan wall lizard** with an olive skin, and the **Italian wall lizard**, a bright olive green with black stripes.

      Wild **tortoises** trundle determinedly around the island, and are more likely to be spotted on walks passing through wooded areas, and on country strolls offering shade and cover.

      You will see many varieties of **butterflies**, **bees**, **beetles** and **snails**, especially in farming areas where uncultivated fields are a riot of wild flowers and grasses.

1. A STROLL AROUND MAÓ

The city of Maó makes the ideal stroll, taking in noble buildings and its magnificent and historic harbour. There are plenty of refreshment stops to tempt you, so regard our time estimate as flexible.

Bus users and car drivers alike begin in **Plaça de s'Esplanada** with its bus terminus and underground pay parking. We cross the square to its north-west side to find the **Tourist Information Office** where you can pick up information about the town and the island. Turning left on leaving the office, we leave the square by the street in its north-eastern corner, **Carrer d'es Negres**. On reaching the T-junction with **Carrer s'Arraval**, we go right.

We take the next street on our left, **Carrer Sant Antoni**, first taking a look at the building on its corner. This is now the **Sala de Cultura**, a venue for shows, exhibitions and concerts although it was once the church of Sant Antoni, Menorca's patron saint. Following the **Carrer Sant Antoni**, we take the second street on our left, **Carrer Sant Jeroni**, which soon leads us into the **Plaça d'es Monestir** with **Església de Sant Francesc** facing us. This church with its ornate baroque façade, thought to have been built in the 17th or 18th centuries, used to be the home of the monks of Saint Francis. To the left of the church stands the **Museu de Menorca**, a museum.

Leaving the square by **Carrer de Isabel 11** opposite the church, we stroll along one of the streets favoured since the 18th century by Menorca's elite. The upper storeys are often the most attractive features of these noble buildings, and you can spot the use of sash windows - an eighteenth century British import and rarely found anywhere else outside the United Kingdom. Look out for houses numbers 58, 60 and 62 whose plaques detail the names and achievements of those who once lived there. About half way along the street is the **Gober Militar**, easily spotted by the sentry posted outside this residence of Menorca's Military Governor. This building was once the home of King Alfonso 111, and the British Governor resided here during Britain's governership of Menorca in the 18th century when Menorca was part of the British Empire.

Towards the end of the street the **Ajuntament** (town hall) marks our arrival at **Plaça de la Constitució**. The town hall dates back as far as 1613 although it was rebuilt in 1788. Look for the English clock set in its wall (donated by Sir Richard Kane, first British Governor of Menorca) to locate the entrance and step inside to see portraits and the coat of arms from Fort St. Philip. Next we take the narrow cobbled lane which runs east from the town hall, **Carrer Alfonso 111** into another square, **Plaça de la Conquista**. On our left is the **Casa Cultural** (formerly Casa Mercadal) dating from 1761 and was the home of one of Menorca's noblest families, constructed on the foundations of a castle. Now a cultural centre, it houses the public library, archives and an art gallery. The square is also occupied by **Església Santa María** and a statue of

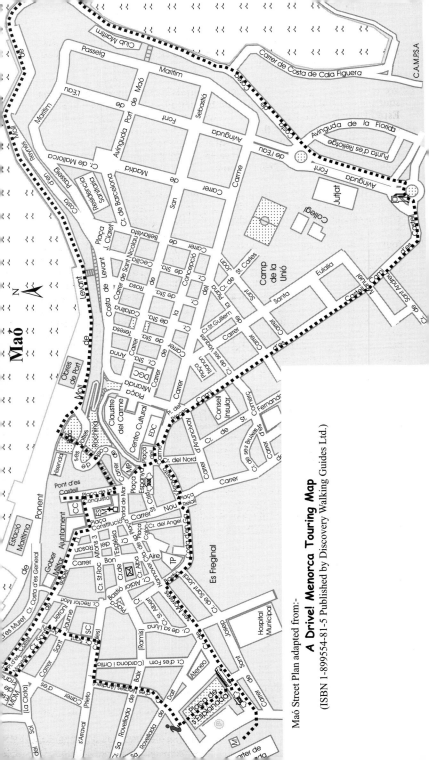

Maó

Maó Street Plan adapted from:-

A Drive! Menorca Touring Map

(ISBN 1-899554-81-5 Published by Discovery Walking Guides Ltd.)

King Alfonso 111 as a young man. Follow **Carrer Alfonso 111** along the few metres to its easternmost end from where there are excellent views of **Maó** harbour from under the **Pont d'es Castell**.

We retrace our steps into **Plaça de la Conquista** and turn left to leave the square on its southern side. Going straight ahead soon brings us into **Plaça Espanya** where we take the steps down on our left into **Parc Rochina**, continuing down through the park to reach the road running around the harbour. It's worth spending time to stroll along and be tempted by one of the many bars and restaurants along the waterfront from where we can admire one of the world's most magnificent harbours.

Follow the harbour road around the **Moll de Levant** as it takes us east and then south, passing the **Club Maritim**. Shortly after where the road forks, we go right on **Costa de Correa** which brings us to a roundabout adorned with an anchor. We walk south along **Avinguda Font de l'Eau** as far as the next roundabout, first passing the law courts (**Jutjat**) on our right. Crossing over, we follow the **Camí d'es Castell** to the left of the petrol station, which heads west and then north-west towards the heart of the town. Staying on this long, almost straight street, we pass the **Consell Insular** (Island Council) building on our left just before entering **Plaça del Príncep**, a small square which leads us into the more imposing **Plaça del Carme**. The convent of the Carmelite nuns, built in 1751, is the massive baroque building which immediately catches the attention, no longer occupied by nuns but housing shops in the basement and ground floors and a cultural centre on the upper floor. Make a detour from **Plaça del Carme** to the adjoining square on its north-west corner, **Plaça Espanya**, if you would like to see the town's fish market, **Mercat Peixanteria**.

Leaving **Plaça del Carme** by its south-west corner on **s'Arravaleta** brings us through **Plaça Reial**, a small but attractive square, and ahead onto **Costa d'en Ga**. As this street angles right its name changes to **Carrer Bastió** and we look out for the old opera house on our right, built in 1824, the **Teatro Principal**. This Italian-designed theatre was created for the British troops during colonial times. Once past the theatre, turn left at the next crossroads on **Carrer de ses Moreres** which soon leads us back to our start point at **Plaça de s'Esplanada**. But before leaving the town, notice the barracks (**Quarter de s'Esplanada**) dating back to the British occupation, and the Monument to the dead of Spain's Civil War (**Monumento**) which stands in the square.

2. FROM TOWN TO TOWN

This walking route has a little bit of everything; ancient city, deep water harbour, small settlement and a hidden entrance into the countryside.

Our starting point is in the bustling **Plaça Esplanade** of **Maó**, ringed by bus termini and very busy on market days. From the north-east corner of the *plaça* we take the **Carrer Morares**, a one-way street lined with small shops. We stay on this main street, making slow progress through the crowds of tourists until we come to a T-junction with **Carrer Bastió Costa Deia**. Here we leave the traffic behind but not the crowds, to go straight over the junction onto the pedestrianised **Carrer de Hannover**. We head steeply downhill between the shops and crowds, towards the **Santa María** church. The narrow street opens out into the small **Plaça Colón** with its statues and drinking taps, before dropping down beside the impressive church. As we come to the end of the street we have a choice of routes; our longer waterfront stroll, or a short cut through the narrow streets of the old town.

SHORT CUT

At the end of **Carrer de Hannover** we go right and follow the traffic past the fish market (*Mercado Pescado*) and climb up to the **Plaça de Carmé**. Crossing over and keeping on the left hand side brings us to the **Carrer de Carmé**. This narrow street is lined by old but rather featureless houses, and we stroll down to meet a modern road at a junction that has a bank (*caixa*) on its corner. From the junction we can see the main road roundabout, a hundred metres away on our right. We go straight over the road onto **Passeig Maritim**. As the *passeig* swings left we come to a path on our right leading through a gap in the concrete wall. Through the wall, the path branches, one section going left to a small park while we go down the steep concrete steps on the right. The concrete stair takes us down past an electricity sub-station to emerge onto **Carrer de Costa Correa**. Turning left, we go down the steep street to the waterfront junction where we rejoin our main route.

STRAIGHT ON

Emerging from the **Carrer de Hannover**, we go straight over the road to a wide stairway. Flights of stairs take us down through this public park, crossing the zigzagging road to bring us onto the harbour by the modern sculptures **(53.469N 16.080E)**. Across the road again, we are at the departure dock for boat excursions. We turn right at the waterfront to stroll past the port administration offices for a couple of minutes before our route comes up alongside the main road. It is easy walking on this part of the walk even though there are still plenty of tourists, as we pass **La Minerva** floating bar/restaurant and the small boats moored along the quayside. We come along to **Maó**'s 'mermaid' statue and head towards the **Il Porto** restaurant. Gradually the tourist crowds thin out as we swing right **(53.510N 16.634E)** to

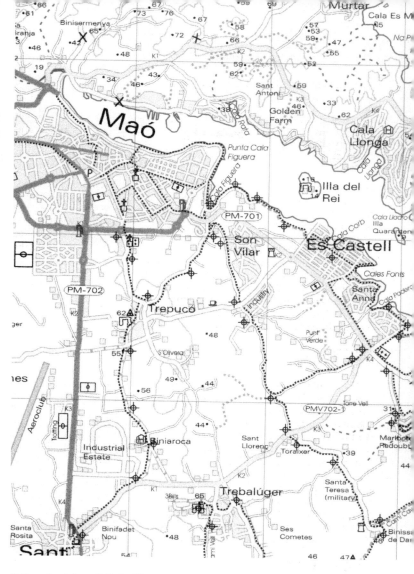

follow the inlet of **Cala Figuera** away from the main harbour. More easy strolling takes us past the **Club Maritimo** and an impressive staired ascent up to the **Passeig Maritima** before meeting our short-cut route at **Restaurant Jagarro (53.298N 16.547E)**.

We go onto the narrow road - don't walk through the boat repair yard as it is a dead end. The road goes gently uphill and swings right around a limestone promontory. Immediately the nature of our route changes, and there is now just the odd local boat and no tourists as we walk along beneath the limestone ridge to the head of **Cala Figuera (53.130N 16.549E)**. At the head of the inlet the road goes inland while we continue on a narrow lane to pass in front of the CHL depot. We swing around the head of the inlet to look back on our earlier route, as we stroll past **Apartamentos Cala Figuera**. On our right is a limestone ridge, and we come to the end of the inlet and swing right (**53.259N 16.750E**), the nature of the walk abruptly changing once again, this time from limestone to the terraced buildings of this small settlement which faces the harbour. Continuing along the lane we pass **Bistro 44**, **Hostal Miramar** and finally **Restaurant Miramar.**

As we approach the end of the settlement the lane narrows where a building stands on the seaward side of our route. Ahead we see the lane curve left to finish in a slipway by a dilapidated building. Undeterred by this sight, we continue on towards two mature trees hiding an electricity sub-station. The house numbers count down to Nº15, where we leave the tarmac to climb a flight of concrete stairs (**53.188N 16.917E**). We swing left on the stairs to continue up past a green-doored house. Pushing our way through wild fig branches, we come up to **Las Gavinas**, complete with its own coat of arms. A few metres on, the concrete path finishes at **Casa Burnet** and we continue on a small path that climbs through a stone wall.

We come into a small meadow which our faint trail crosses and then climbs up a stone slope to a junction. From the junction, we take the main trail which follows the line of the harbour's cliffs. After the mostly urban nature of our walk so far, we now find ourselves in an abundant sea of wild flowers which push in on our route. We walk along the top of the cliffs alongside an old stone wall, breached occasionally to give *mirador* viewing points over the harbour. On our right, the stone-walled fields have been taken over by verdant wild plants, as our trail cuts through the walls to come to an isolated cove opposite **Illa del Rei (53.074N 17.103E)**, once used as an isolation hospital. Here the trail drops steeply down to the left, requiring a little clambering before it climbs onto the clifftop plateau again. After a few metres the trail leaves the cliff edge to head towards the pink apartment block which marks the edge of **Es Castell**.

The trail brings us onto a tarmac road which takes us through this quiet area, swinging right past some new houses and climbing up to a road junction beside an electricity sub-station. Turning left, we go gently downhill past streets off to our right until we reach **Carrer Bon-Air** just before a steep lane goes down to our left. We turn onto **Carrer Bon-Air** and follow it to its end at a T-junction overlooking **Cala Corb (52.964N 17.444E)**. We go left and come to a gap in the concrete wall where a steep concrete stair takes us down to sea level. Walking up to the head of the inlet, we pass **Bar Picatapas** which makes a pleasant refreshment stop. We ignore the road out of the inlet and take a narrow concrete stair by the sign **Moli de Cala Corb** which climbs steeply to the cliff top where we emerge into a little square at the end of **Carrer de Cales Fonts**. Just a few metres along its route **Carrer de Cales Fonts** opens out into **Plaça de S'Esplanada (52.867N 17.494E)**, a former parade ground for the old army barracks which faces the square. There are bars and cafés in the *plaça* but for more stylish refreshment you should go one street inland to **Carrer Gran**. This is **Es Castell**'s main shopping, eating and drinking street offering a good choice of hostelries during peak tourist season.

3. GUARDS, GUARDS!

The entrance to **Maó** harbour has to be one of the most 'battlemented' pieces of ground in the Mediterranean, as successive occupiers attempted to hold off the next group of invaders. On this easy walk we touch upon two major forts and a watchtower, before finishing on the fortified watchtower of **Torre d'en Penyat**. From the *torre* you have the option of an alternative return route to **Cala de Sant Esteve**, or of taking Walk 4, 'Escape From The Tower' to produce a circular route back to **Es Castell**. If you choose to stop at the watchtower and limestone phenomena, this is only a 'two walker' route.

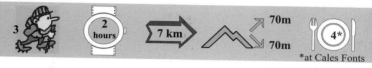

3   2 hours   7 km   70m / 70m   4*

*at Cales Fonts

We start in the barrack square **(52.867N 17.494E)**, **Plaça de S'Esplanada** of **Es Castell**, and take the **Carrer de Cales Fonts** on the eastern side of the square. **La Mahonesa** store is on the corner of the street. A short stroll down this terraced street brings us onto **Carrer de Sa Font** overlooking the picturesque bay of **Cales Fonts (52.799N 17.644E)**. Here we have a choice of routes; we can go left to walk past the **Club Maritim** restaurant, or turn right to go down to the seafront restaurants on the **Moll de Cala Fonts**. Former fishermen's lock-ups have been converted into stylish eateries and 'arty' shops as tourism takes over from fishing. At the end of the bay we walk up from the glass-bottom boat dock to come onto **Carrer Sant Josep**. Of course, we could have simply turned right to circle above the restaurants to join **Carrer Sant Josep** by the public water fountain.

Carrer Sant Josep goes steadily uphill to bring us up to the main road **(52.560N 17.579E)** between **Bar Sa Sasina** on our left and the bus stop on our right. We go left to stroll along the broad pavement and climb past the **El Italiano** restaurant on the crest of the road. Stone-walled fields, mostly abandoned, and old farmhouses make up the right-hand landscape, along with an old aqueduct supported on stone and concrete pillars. The old farmhouse of **Son Calapat** contrasts with new villas, as we drop down into a shallow valley. A gentle uphill section brings us up to the **Sol del Este** road junction **(52.315N 17.788E)** where Walk 4, 'Escape From The Tower' comes down the main road on our right to cross our route.

We continue straight ahead on a minor tarmac lane, leaving the traffic noise behind us as we pass the cemetery. Around us is a quiet rural landscape of small fields with stone walls, as we walk towards the gates of a military camp. Before we reach the gates we turn right **(52.209N 17.938E)** to walk down a narrow lane between shoulder-high walls. Ahead is the round tower of **Torre d'en Penyat** as we stroll along between fields, and the lane starts to run downhill to overlook the cove of **Cala de Sant Esteve**. At a battered traffic sign **(51.938N 18.023E)**, a lane goes down to our right - see Walk 3B, 'The Roman Way' for an alternative route down into the cove.

We stay on the narrow lane for a relaxed descent, taking a short break to walk out amongst the TV aerials on a limestone table for a picturesque view of this beautiful inlet. The lane brings us down to the first houses set against the limestone cliffs, a complete change of scene impossible to imagine from our rural plateau five minutes earlier. This idyllic settlement (yachties' heaven) is set around the inlet; look out for architectural novelties such as tree-branch railings and art-deco water downpipes as we circle around the head of the inlet. One blackspot, a large but incomplete villa almost overgrown by blackberry bushes, marks our alternative return route. We come to a drinks machine along the lane, the only refreshments available during the route. Gently climbing, we come to an old well behind a public telephone, before reaching the tunnel entrance to the **Marlborough Redoubt (51.901N 18.190E)** although unfortunately, the gates are chained shut! Across the cove from us is a military recreation area fashioned out of the seaward side of **Fort Sant Felipe (Castell de San Felipe)**, as we walk below **Villa Theresa** towards the mouth of the inlet.

Sharp limestone marks the inlet's entrance as the lane swings right to bring us to an unusual geological formation. Alongside a mini football pitch, limestone flats and steps run out to the sea's edge. This is not a natural phenomenon; the original limestone cliffs were cut into blocks to build the fortifications in this area, resulting in this strange 'geology'. We climb up to the end of the lane in front of **Villa Katty (51.826N 18.304E)** and take a faint trail across to the fortified watchtower. At the first entrance to the tower we find a stone toilet! Continuing round the tower, we find a pair of green doors which open to reveal the relatively modern trappings of a recent dwelling within the tower.

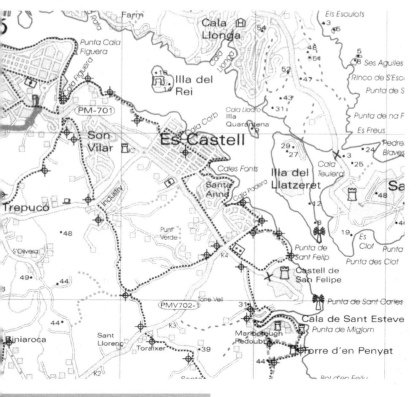

From the watchtower, a narrow trail with stone steps leads us to the highest levels of rock cutting. Keeping right, we come to a room-like area where a faint trail can be seen climbing the 'steps'. A little climb brings us up to follow the trail through a stone wall, and wild flowers and butterflies abound as our path heads across abandoned fields towards the round tower. We follow the trail down around a jagged limestone outcrop, to cross stone walls and reach a great rent in the cliffs. Here, the seaward cliff has split away and shifted two metres towards the sea. From the rent, we pass a neat water run-off tunnel formed in an old stone wall before coming to a fork in the path. We stay on the main path which climbs gently towards the tower, passing through a wall and the remains of a cottage to come to another fork in the path. Again we continue towards the tower, crossing a stone wall to come into an area of huge irregular limestone boulders. Below the *torre* is another junction of faint trails where Walk 4, 'Escape from the Tower' and Walk 3A, 'Camí de Cavalls' go right in front of the entrance to a square cave, rather 'garage' like and occasionally used to pen goats. We go left to pick our way up towards the entrance to the round tower **(51.709N 18.340E)**.

Steel steps with partly corroded hand rails give access into the tower. We emerge into a circular room with domed roof - take care not to fall down the steps to your left, just inside. The acoustics of this room are remarkable, adding volume and resonance to every spoken word. By the entrance tunnel, a steep spiral stairway leads up to the roof of **Torre d'en Penyat**, from where we have outstanding views over the region. In contrast with this historical area, two palatial new villas have been built to the west of the tower, their style differing starkly from the traditional 'stepped stone' shed below the first villa. **Torre d'en Penyat** has a chequered history, the stories varying depending upon whom you listen to. Built during the Napoleonic Wars (1797) after **Fort de Sant Felipe** was demolished, it was known as the execution tower where miscreants were hanged. From the *torre* we have the choice of returning the way we came, using our slightly more vigorous Walk 3A return, or taking Walk 4 for a very different return to **Es Castell**.

3A. CAMÍ DE CAVALLS

Here we take an alternative return route from the tower to **Cala de Sant Esteve** using the **Camí de Cavalls**. This ancient donkey trail runs down the east coast of Menorca, but in recent years has become very neglected and overgrown in places. Other sections of the **Camí de Cavalls** feature in our Walk 4, 'Escape From The Tower', and Walk 11, 'From The New To The Old'.

We start outside the 'garage' like cave below the *torre* where Walk 3 goes right and Walk 4 swings left. Here, we go straight ahead on the faint path to pass through a gap in the stone wall. Another couple of metres, and we are crossing another wall before the faint trail meanders across the meadows in the general direction of **Cala de Sant Esteve**. Through another wall and diagonally across a meadow, our path curves left around pistacia bushes to go through 'Snake Gap' (as it was here that Ros met a large golden-brown snake). We go gently up across another meadow and past a mound of stones on our left towards a gap in a very broken-down stone wall covered in pistacia bushes. The faint path curves right through yet another wall **(51.750N 18.104E)**, actually the double walls of an old donkey trail jammed full of pistacias. We loop across the corner of a field, another faint trail joining us from the right, to go through a stone wall. The trail has become a wide path as we head away from the coast to come onto the **Camí de Cavalls** donkey trail (no signs).

Uphill from us the **Camí de Cavalls** is completely choked with bushes, up to the point where Walk 4 comes onto the donkey trail. We turn right to follow the old trail downhill on a mixture of limestone slabs and laid boulders. It is steadily downhill on the easy but uneven trail, until we are almost above **Cala de Sant Esteve**. Here, the trail gets steeper and rougher as it drops down to the left to run below limestone cliffs. Plants push in on the trail to reduce it to a narrow walking track as we come down to a sign, '**Camí de Cavalls**' set in the cliffs. The path turns sharp right, coming down alongside a house and then emerging onto a tarmac road alongside an abandoned villa project.

3B. A ROMAN ROAD

As we approach **Cala de Sant Esteve** on the tarmac road, we start going downhill at a 30km sign, and a few metres on is a corroded Z-bend sign, alongside which is a dirt lane. Taking the dirt lane, we soon find that it narrows to a cobbled trail, reputedly dating from Roman times. The trail goes steeply down to swing right past caves, and then runs beneath a huge boulder supported by loose rocks. We go down through an S-bend to come alongside a high stone-block wall. Some paths go off left towards the houses and an *ermita* below us, as we round a corner of the wall and continue dropping down for our trail to emerge on the tarmac lane at the very head of the inlet.

CALA DE SANT ESTEVE

These days, this idyllic little cove exudes a peaceful and charming atmosphere. But it was not always like this; the strategic importance of this narrow inlet at the mouth of Maó's great harbour meant that for centuries, Cala de Sant Esteve has played an important part in Menorca's colourful history.

The remains of Fort de Sant Felipe, built in 1554 and destroyed in the late eighteenth century, stand on the south side of the harbour mouth. On the other side, in far better repair, is the British built Marlborough Redoubt, a seven-sided structure intended to complement Fort de Sant Felipe. It is even rumored that an underwater passageway used to link the two fortifications.

4. ESCAPE FROM THE TOWER

This walk cannot be completed on its own; we have included this route for those walkers who want to extend Walk 3, 'Guards, Guards!' with this interesting country stroll back to **Es Castell** /**Cales Fonts** by a very different route. By using our secateurs we have made the **Camí de Cavalls** donkey trail section reasonably passable. After this section we stroll through idyllic rural countryside followed by modern villas, to finish in the waterfront restaurants at **Cales Fonts**. This description alone should make it worth completing Walk 3, so that you can reach the start of this walk.

We start by following Walk 3, 'Guards, Guards!', down from the tower to the front of the 'garage' cave. Here we take the faint trail to a corner of the meadow where the wall is broken down. We now keep parallel to the newer stone wall on our left and walk across open grounds and walls, to a gap in the walls of the donkey trail ahead of us. Don't be tempted to follow a small trail heading diagonally across the meadows which leads to a 'pallet' gate and onto private farmland - walkers not welcome! Through the wall, we come onto the **Camí de Cavalls** donkey trail **(51.629N 18.139E)**, impassable to our right but merely overgrown as we turn left to push through the foliage. We go steadily uphill between the high walls, cutting back bushes and brambles as we go, to emerge after five minutes between a new house and the massive entrance of the villa we saw from the tower. If the villa's gates are open you will notice how much smaller **Torre d'en Penyat** seems from this viewpoint.

We have emerged onto a dirt road **(51.433N 18.129E)** and stroll down from the villa's entrance past 'weekender' smallholdings. Ignoring a dirt road on our right, we continue down the dirt road in the direction of an old fortified farmhouse. Our route swings right past more weekender homes such as **Bon Antonia** (built 1988 and extended in 1996), and we pass a lane off to our left. Staying on the dirt road as it passes through this almost urban area, we come up to a junction signed 'Huertos de Binissaida' **(51.290N 17.897E)** back the way we have come, and 'Horts de Binissaida' on the route joining us from **S'Algar**. We go right on the narrow lane, now tarmacked, to stroll down past the military compound of **Santa Teresa** to the entrance of **Sant Joán de Binissaida**. A more thoughtful owner of this farm might have encouraged an easy, direct route from the tower, but it seems that Menorca's 'siege mentality' lives on.

We pass the 'control tower' for the military radio aerials and climb up a small rise to a restored farmhouse. The lane loops round the farmhouse, **Ses Obatones**, to wriggle its way through this market gardening area. Intriguing (though private) trails lead off our route, as we follow the narrow lane between small stone-walled fields. We come along to an old cottage opposite a large farmhouse. The lane takes a 90° turn to the right and passes a tiled threshing circle (no longer in use) before reaching the farm's entrance (**Toraixa des Pi**) with its marble tiled seat. At a new bungalow the lane swings

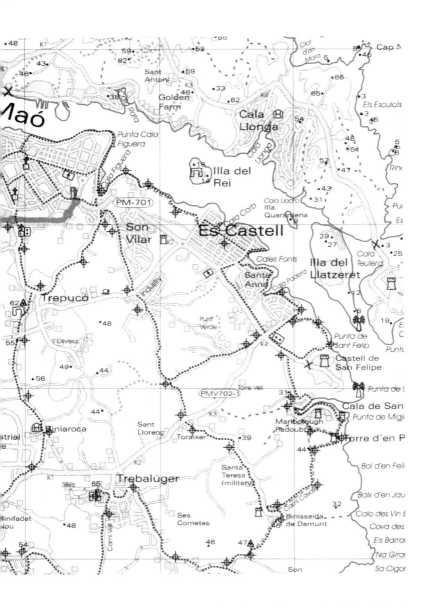

right, while we continue straight ahead to walk past the old traditional farmhouses and reach the PMV702-1 main road **(51.819N 17.190E)**.

Watching out for traffic on this tricky bend, we cross straight over the main road onto a dirt lane. Bored guard dogs noisily welcome visitors, as we stroll down past new houses. After these impressive country residences the lane narrows and the vegetation pushes in on the lane, only occasionally beaten back by a passing vehicle. We stroll up the lumpy limestone surface (well-cushioned footwear advisable) between stone walls almost overwhelmed by pistacia bushes and blackberry brambles. As the lane levels out we come along to a junction where the route of Walk 6, 'Camí de Biniatap' **(52.042N 17.067E)**, joins us from the left.

At the junction we go right to walk along an even narrower lane heading towards **Binimaimo**. Through a tree-lined section, we pass the entrances to weekender houses on our left and pass through an S-bend, unfortunately notable for its smelly pig-runs. The lane wriggles along between fields of pasture and stone-built cattle huts, as we head towards a bleak industrial building. After a gentle downhill we walk up past the disused rural factory to find the much more interesting **Binimaimo** farmhouse on our left. We come to modern houses hidden behind high fences, and swing left to the rather gruesome sight of an abandoned and vandalised cemetery. Rubbish 'dumpsters' stand outside the old cemetery, and we come onto a tarmac lane **(52.202N 17.554E)**, which we walk down to join the PMV702-1 main road **(52.247N 17.690E)**. Watching out for traffic, we walk downhill on the main road to meet the route of Walk 3 at the **Sol del Este** junction **(52.315N 17.788E)**.

If you are in a rush to finish then you can strike off down the main road to **Es Castell**, but we will take a gentle stroll through the seafront developments to **Cales Fonts**. We go straight over the cross-roads to walk down the broad road towards the **Sol del Este** development. It is gently downhill on the potholed road to the start of our Walk 5, 'Silent Guns' route opposite **Carrer Levante** **(52.422N 17.977E)**. We continue down past the **Passeig Maritim** street sign to swing left and find the welcome sight of **Café Sol del Este** ahead of us. From the café we climb up a short rise to pass the **La Gardenia** apartments from where we have views down into **Cala Padera**. We follow the lane towards the head of the inlet until we reach the **Bar Sol Naciente** car park. At the edge of the car park, flights of steps take us down to the small beach at the head of the inlet

Although a path leads around the seaward side of the villas, it ends abruptly in thick undergrowth at the top of the cliffs. Denied a sea route, we climb up the dirt lane from the beach to come to a street, where we turn right to walk around the landward side of the villas, many with well-stocked gardens. We climb up behind the villas overlooking **Cales Fonts** and continue along the street, passing a small square below us on our right before going right to come onto **Carrer Sant Josep**. A short stroll downhill brings us onto the waterfront of **Cales Fonts** with a wide choice of hostelries for refreshment.

5. SILENT GUNS

This interesting short walk is intended to be combined with Walk 3, 'Guards, Guards!' or Walk 4, 'Escape From The Tower'. Although it crosses over private land, we haven't experienced any problems from the landowner, but if you encounter trouble we would advise you to retreat apologetically.

3 | 1 hour | 3 km | 50m / 50m | 0

We start on the route of Walk 4, 'Escape From The Tower' at the edge of **Sol del Este** housing estate **(52.422N 17.977E)**. On the right hand side of the road is a 'ambos lados' traffic sign, opposite the **Carrer Levante**. Just past the sign we can see an interesting path leading through a cornfield down towards the sea. It is a tricky climb over and down from the wall, and with a drop into the field, but it then becomes a very gentle trail. On our right are 'garage' style caves created by the cutting of limestone used in the construction of the forts in this area. Just how much limestone was cut to create these fortifications becomes apparent when you realise that the whole depression containing this sunken field was once solid limestone, up at the level of the road!

The clear path leads across the cornfield to follow a stone wall down towards the harbour mouth. We come to a gap in the wall, and ignoring the trail going right, we continue down to the foreshore. The trail takes us down around a tiny inlet and towards a walled enclosure which bears the legend, 'Propiedad de l'Armada Española' **(52.376N 18.179E)**. We go through the narrow entrance (no gate) to discover the most modern fortification on the island - a bunker dating from the Spanish Civil War. If you are of a forceful nature and armed with secateurs, you could explore the bunker. We satisfy ourselves with a peek into the barracks from above the blast-resistant entrance channel. Having explored the bunker compound - watch out for big holes alongside the path - we go out the gate and back onto the trail, to pass around the inland side of the wall and go above the bunker's seaward entrance (sealed).

Watch out for more large holes beside the path as we curve right towards the military camp. Just before we reach the camp **(52.376N 18.217E)** our path goes right to climb up beside the fence. We stroll across the meadows, following the faint path before climbing up alongside the military monument. The path continues parallel to the fence until we reach a corner of the encampment where the path goes across to a gap in the stone wall. We come into a cornfield and swing left to follow its edge to the **Bateria San Felipe** guard tower, where we go right to walk along to the field entrance. We come onto the tarmac lane at the junction where our Walk 3, 'Guards, Guards!' route goes down to **Cala Sant Esteve (52.209N 17.938E)**. The final section is an easy stroll to the **Sol del Este** junction, where we turn right and stroll down to our start point.

6. CAMÍ DE BINIATAP

Around **Maó**, you could get the impression that the car and modern road developments have obliterated the old donkey trails. While this is true of many routes, this walk takes us on the route of an old *camino* which, despite a few bits of tarmac, is much the same as in the old days when it was a main trail into **Maó**.

3   1 or 2 hours   3 or 7 km   50m / 50m   0

(The shorter distance and time applies to the point where this walk joins Walk 4, 'Escape From The Tower'.
Follow the longer distance and time to reach **Es Castell/Cales Fonts** by following the final section of Walk 4.)

Our starting point is on the main road at the head of **Cala Figuera** on the outskirts of **Maó (53.059N 16.549E)**. Across the main road from the bay is a wide, but virtually unused, new road. We walk up this new road for one hundred and fifty metres, then go left onto a dirt lane. The lane curves up under limestone cliffs and caves to come up behind the advertising hoardings which overlook the main road. Our route swings right to climb up past the '**Camí de Biniatap**' sign set on a stone-block wall. It is a steady climb up the rough limestone rock lane and into the countryside. The lane levels out as we approach the **Son Vilar** housing development and continue along to come out on a tarmac parking area **(52.949N 16.690E)**. Keeping the houses on our left, we walk up to another parking area from where our donkey trail heads off into the countryside.

The trail runs between fields to come alongside an unusual fortress tower with an external staircase, just before we reach another edge of the **Son Vilar** development. We come onto a narrow dirt lane between a farm entrance and the garages of **Papallona**. The older houses of **Son Vilar** line the left of our route, as we come to another fortress tower with an external staircase. From close to it appears that the towers are part of the water distribution system for the area. The lane becomes tarmacked where a concrete lane goes off to our left, and we walk comfortably up past an old farmhouse to a junction with the PM 710-1 **Es Castell - Trepucó** road **(52.563N 16.798E)**.

Crossing over the road, we continue on the narrow tarmac lane to pass an electricity sub-station and come to the interface of modern industry and rural agriculture; **Es Castell**'s small industrial estate comes up the lane to face the old farmhouse of **Los Torreleros**. We continue on past cottages and come to a street signed **Carrer de Fusters** going left, where we go straight on to meet a junction of the lane in front of a stone wall. Some maps show this left hand lane as a right of way through to **Binimaimo**, but unfortunately this interesting route, elevated above the countryside, ends in a walled meadow behind the impassable wall of a chicken farm.

Taking the right hand lane at the junction, we go past a 'leaping deer' street

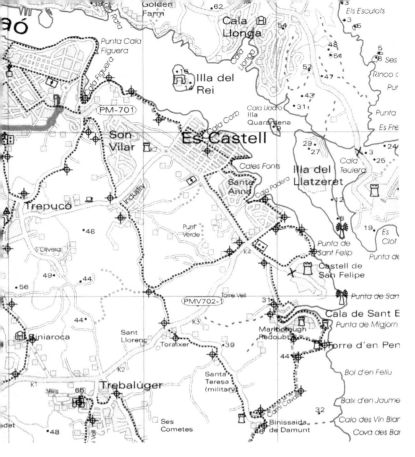

sign as the lane reverts to a rough limestone surface. Our route takes us past the **Nusa** farmhouse, and the lane twists behind more large farmhouses and narrows to barely a car's width. In the unlikely event of meeting a car on this section of the route (although we were passed by a diminutive Fiat 500) you'll need to press yourself against the wall. We stroll gently downhill between walls overgrown with blackberries and pistacia bushes, the lane weaving its way through the tranquil rural landscape. An extensive farm sits below the lane on our left, just before trees and bushes restrict our views. The lane gets even narrower as the stone walls give way to trees and a farm plot lined by bamboo, just before coming to a junction marked by substantial new field entrances.

We have come out onto the route of Walk 4, 'Escape From The Tower' **(52.042N 17.067E)**. Ahead, the lane leads on to the farmsteads of **Toraixer**, although if you are looking forward to some refreshments, we suggest you go left to follow Walk 4 down to **Cales Fonts** at **Es Castell.**

7. UP TO TREPUCÓ

Usually we avoid traffic routes and keep to country trails whenever possible, but here we make an exception with a choice of two easy routes on quiet lanes from **Maó** to the archaeological site at **Trepucó**.

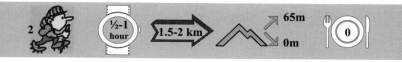

2 | ½-1 hour | 1.5-2 km | 65m 0m | 0

A. From Cala Figuera

Our starting point is on the main road at the head of **Cala Figuera** on the outskirts of **Maó** (as in Walk 6, 'C a m í   d e   B i n i a t a p') (**5 3 . 0 5 9 N 16.549E**). Across the main road from the bay is a wide but virtually unused new road. We take this road and continue along the tarmac, ignoring the dirt lane on our left. The broad entrance to the road soon narrows down as we walk steadily up to pass massively walled terraces which line the canyon on our right. Limestone caves border the left side of our road as we continue to climb steadily up out of the canyon. The road passes **Cinea Maxtania** and levels out to a more gentle gradient, for us to stroll along past abandoned fields and huts. Past a traffic sign for a junction, we pass a trail off on our left, 100 metres before coming up to the 'main road' and the **Talaiot Trepucó** sign (**52.572N 16.087E**).

Across the main road, we walk along a narrow lane which twists round a farmhouse between high walls. We come to a limestone-cobbled trail on our right which we follow to cover the last few metres into the site - look out for the large cave at the start of this little lane **(52.506N 15.989E)**.

Trepucó dates back some 3,000 years, and is a large walled site with standing stones as well as the *talaiot*. It boasts the tallest *taula* on Menorca, at a height of 4 metres. From the walls (added in 1782), we can see what appears to be a smaller *talaiot* or *naveta* across a cornfield, though not accessible from this site. You soon have to become used to the lack of catering at archaeological sites, so we recommend our Walk 8, 'On To A Hostelry' route to **La Rueda** in **Sant Lluís** as a follow-on walk through beautiful countryside, which also offers refreshments.

B. From Plaça Esplanada

Starting in the **Plaça Esplanada**, we leave by the western corner on **Carrer de Moreres**. Yes, it does seem like the wrong direction, but in a few metres we come to the first junction and turn right onto **Carrer Cos de Garcia**, now going in the right direction. We stroll along the length of the street to come to the **Maó** ring road, **Via de Ronda (52.992N 15.917E)**.

Taking care crossing the dual carriageway, we go straight over the ring road onto the lane signed **Talaiot de Trepucó**. We walk up past the cemetery on this quiet lane, passing a lane **(52.835N 15.938E)** and another sign to **Talaiot de Trepucó**. Our lane winds its way around traditional farmhouses to pass the entrance of **Los Dos Pins** on our right. It's an easy stroll past cultivated terraces, before the lane twists uphill in front of a wide concrete road. We come up to a junction to follow the **Talaiot de Trepucó** sign along **Camí d'en Verd**. The narrow lane twists its way along between high stone walls, and in a few metres we come to the limestone lane which takes us past a large ground-level cave and into the archaeological site **(52.506N 15.989E)**.

THE PUZZLE OF THE *TAULAS*

You will see these table-like stone slabs in many locations across Menorca. But what were they for? Experts have come up with theories but no conclusive proof so far. They are always found in settlements and stand inside a part-circle of standing stones. Perhaps they played a part in religious rituals, or were a kind of totem; maybe they were used in ancient studies of the heavens. Another theory suggests that these massive stone structures represented the head of a bull.

8. ON TO A HOSTELRY

Trepucó and its *taula* and *talaiot* are impressive and memorable, but there are no refreshments, neither at the site nor in the hamlet. This would be reason enough for us to search for a country route to a hostelry, and if you add a narrow country lane running through beautiful countryside, you have our 'On To A Hostelry' route. Unfortunately the last kilometre has to be on the main road into **Sant Lluís**, but don't let this dissuade you.

1 | 1 hour | 3 km | 20m ↗ 40m ↘ | 3

Walking back down the rough limestone lane from the archaeological site at **Trepucó**, we come onto the narrow tarmac lane. We follow the traffic sign and turn right to stroll along the narrow lane past the *talaiot*, coming to a group of traditional farmhouses where the lane opens out. A few metres on, passing the terrace which includes the pink **Villa Rosenado**, we come to a main lane **(52.314N 15.960E)**.

We go straight over the cross-roads, the lane here quite wide, and walk past an old house on our left and a pair of newer terraced houses on our right. The lane narrows as we come past an unusual new building and an electricity sub-station, to go gently downhill. Dry stone walls press in on us as we walk along to a monument topped with a cross.

On reaching the monument we find that its drinking fountain has long ceased to function and any inscriptions have been weathered away, but we do get good views from its

steps, looking out over the countryside to the forts and prison near the entrance to **Maó** harbour. Now the lane swings left and we stroll gently downhill between fallow fields, the lane opening out as we come to a cluster of country houses. Past the houses, we come to a junction **(51.704N 16.181E)** and again follow the traffic instructions by taking the lane to the right. We pass a large villa on our left as the lane narrows, and then walk past a smallholding with a breeze-block wall, just before our route wriggles its way onto the main road **(51.517N 16.061E)**.

Sant Lluís is in sight as we walk in single file down the main road to drop down into a shallow valley. We come up a gentle gradient to meet the first houses of this small town. The road goes through S-bends between traditional cottages (Menorcan traffic calming? Take care on this section.) to bring us up to a main road junction, opposite the BP petrol station **(51.226N 15.629E)**.

We carefully cross over the main road and take the little street, **Bisbe Sever**, to come to a public square. Across the square and to the windmill brings us onto the main street of **Sant Lluís**, **Carrer Sant Lluís**. We turn left to see the welcome sight of red and green drinks signs, indicating hostelries. Walking down the street, we reach the first of these, **Bar/Restaurant La Rueda**, a bustling establishment popular with the locals, and with air conditioning - most welcome on a hot summer's day **(51.125N 15.576E)**.

SANT LLUÍS

After taking refreshments in Sant Lluís, take time to wander around the streets of this attractive little town, founded in 1761 to provide housing for French troops, in occupation of Menorca at that time. The imposing white, buttressed church displays the coats of arms of the French royal family and also that of the first French governor of Menorca, the Comte de Lannion.

On the north side of the town stands the Molí de Dalt, a working windmill housing a folk museum which is open to the public (limited opening in winter, daily but not Sundays in summer), displaying farm tools and equipment from previous generations.

9. LINKING THE RESORTS

Menorca's southern resorts, from **Binibèquer Vell** to **Punta Prima**, were once linked by a coastal trail. Development has resulted in much of this route becoming tarmacked road with good pavements, which does make for easy strolling and requires few directions. For the final stage from **Biniancolla** to **Punta Prima** we take a coastal path, although even here there is an easier though less interesting tarmac lane alternative, which would reduce the 'walker' rating from three to two.

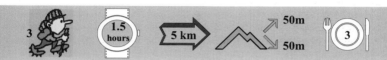

We leave **Binibèquer Vell**'s commercial centre **(49.443N 13.870E)**, set in the quaint reproduction 'Menorcan Fishing Village' development, and follow the coastal road's wide pavement eastwards. Through the resort areas of **Binibèquer Vell** and **Binibèquer Nou**, the rule is to follow the road, keeping right (or straight on) **(49.187N 14.232E)** at any junction, with the exceptions of private entries or cul-de-sacs. Just over a kilometre of easy strolling, and we are overlooking the white sands and azure seas of **Cala Binibèquer**, described by some holiday reps as "a beach in a Caribbean setting" - where do they get them from? Trails lead down to the beach, as we follow the road down into the valley behind the beach, and up past a car park to continue on the coastal road **(49.111N 14.811E)**.

At **Cala de Torret** we can take a diversion from the main road for a while by going right at the information sign with letters missing. We go down a street of boat garages to the tiny dock where we take a tarmac lane to our left. Passing a vehicle barrier, we come above the limestone shore and a pair of islands to come down into **Cala de Torret** proper. The lane drops down into the bay where we turn left on **Passeig des Porxos**, a tiled promenade lined with boat garages. We follow the *passeig* along the bay until the red tiling swings left by house Nº55. Here, we continue straight ahead on a dirt track which serves the villas on the far side of the inlet. Past a traditional boat garage and below **La Familia**, the path runs along in front of the villas. We return to the coastal road by any of the access paths on our left.

From **Cala de Torret** it is easy strolling on pavements to the edge of **Biniancolla.** Here the main road swings inland as we go right, into the village, to come to **Restaurant Biniancolla** and walk down the street across the head of the inlet. At Nº39 the street turns right to go uphill past villas which line the inlet. We continue on the street until it swings left, and an open cul-de-sac is ahead of us. If you want to take the easier route to **Punta Prima** then follow the street which runs behind the coastal villas. We go down the cul-de-sac to turn left in front of a small villa built on a grass mound **(48.713N 15.852E)**. At the **Villa Nevara** we follow the faint walking trail which runs along between the villas and the limestone shoreline. It is gently uphill on the faint and uneven trail, until we come to the unusual villa of circles, with a shower at its apex. The trail now goes down in front of **Restaurant Son Ganzo** to a set of

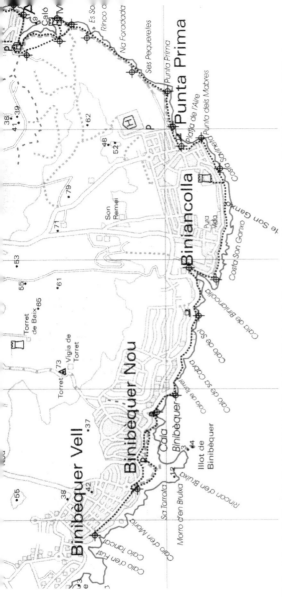

villas in the twilight of their useful lives, a sharp inlet cutting into the coastline on our right. A pavement runs in front of the villas before we revert to the dirt trail which brings us up to an area of new developments.

The path is interrupted by the recent developments, but looking ahead we can see its continuation running around the seaward side of a villa. Going around the new villas brings us back onto the trail - note that there are no villas on the seaward side of this route - to climb up onto the headland. The coastal path skirts the villas as it runs along above the sharply jagged coastline, until we come to a major inlet. Here, the trail climbs up to a tarmac street to cross the inlet, and after the stone wall above the inlet, or at the first street light on the right, we go back down to the coastal track. Our track passes more jagged inlets before coming to the front door of a small villa faced with natural stone, where we begin the most geologically interesting part of our route.

We step out onto horizontal limestone tables which form a flat walking route. On our left, the limestone has been weathered into a variety of shapes which show the thin, layered construction of the rock. Across the tabletop, the level on which we are walking now continues as a series of small, flat steps - be careful with your footing, and remember our advice, 'Look where you walk, and STOP to look at the view!' We come round to wider limestone tabletops and a pair of large boulders to overlook the beach at **Punta Prima (48.770N 16.910E)**. The final stage is an easy stroll down the street, and not quite as easy across the sand (you could loop round on the road) to the beach front bars for some refreshment **(48.916N 16.882E)**.

10. COASTAL DISCOVERY

The south-east corner of Menorca, from **Punta Prima** to **Alcalfar** and on to **S'Algar**, offers us one of the unspoilt coastal walks on the island. Combining good scenery, some impressive coastline, an immaculately restored fortified tower and a scenic refreshment stop, (in **Alcalfar**) this route is a must for everyone with well cushioned footwear.

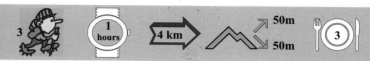

We start our favourite Menorca walk where the **Punta Prima** development stops abruptly at the end of the beach **(48.961N 17.004E)**. Leaving tourism behind us, we stroll along the sandy trail which parallels the limestone-slab shoreline. In a couple of minutes we come to the low walls of the old salt evaporation pans, at the end of which we have a choice of following the main trail inland to a stone wall, or taking the seaward route on a narrow sandy path. The two routes come together on a dirt road which runs alongside a substantial stone wall **(49.122N 17.390E)**. Inland of the wall is a wild, natural landscape, while all along our route you will find excellent specimens of endemic plants which thrive in this natural rock garden. We pass through a stone wall and the trail narrows down to a walking trail which threads its way between the pistacia bushes. Faint paths lead off the main trail down towards the sea as our route becomes rougher.

As our walking trail climbs gently, the limestone-table shoreline is replaced by small cliffs, and we come to water run-off conduits built into the stone wall alongside our route. We follow the limestone track as it moves away from the sea and starts climbing to cross the headland. Limestone boulders are scattered like discarded 'weetabix' on top of the table seashore, as we continue gently climbing up the trail. An immaculate fortified tower comes into view **(49.410N 17.722E)**, and the shoreline becomes more dramatic while we continue climbing up the headland. Before we reach the crest of the headland, a trail heads towards the tower **(49.508N 17.773E)**. Here, we divert onto the minor trail and go towards the **Torre d'Alcalfar Vell**.

Torre d'Alcalfar Vell (49.570N 17.828E) has been so immaculately sanitised that it looks like Hollywood's idea of a tower, very different from the brooding presence of the 'execution tower' on our Walk 3, 'Guards, Guards!' route. Walking around the base of the tower gives us excellent views across the south-east coastline. Leaving the tower, we take a walking trail which heads down towards the small inlet of **Caló Roig**. Our path drops quickly down, assisted by limestone steps, to come above the inlet with its undercut cliffs, the swell of the ocean causing the eroded cliffs to pant like an old dog. We come down alongside **Caló Roig**'s tiny beach **(49.591N 17.701E)** to rejoin the main trail by an ancient well.

We leave **Caló Roig** behind as the trail climbs steadily onto the next headland in a series of limestone 'stairs'. Reaching the crest **(49.761N 17.616E)**, we look down on the beautiful inlet of **Cala d'Alcalfar** and its unusual limestone island with a natural tunnel through its centre. As we start to descend from the

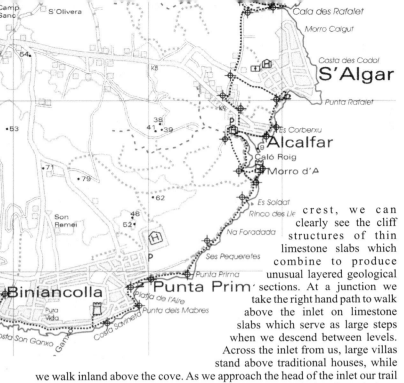

crest, we can clearly see the cliff structures of thin limestone slabs which combine to produce unusual layered geological sections. At a junction we take the right hand path to walk above the inlet on limestone slabs which serve as large steps when we descend between levels. Across the inlet from us, large villas stand above traditional houses, while we walk inland above the cove. As we approach the head of the inlet our trail climbs to join another path and comes into an area of pistacia and cistus bushes. We come down between the mature trees of a small wood to a junction, where we take the right hand route to drop down onto the beach at the head of the cove. Across the sand, and we come onto the terrace of the **Xuroy (49.808N 17.671E)**, our favourite refreshment stop in this region. It would be a crime not to spend a little time here, enjoying a drink at this most scenic of inlets.

After our break at the **Xuroy** we have options of how we link with the path to **S'Algar**, or we can cut through to our Walk 10, 'From The New To The Old'. Today, we take the steep concrete lane which goes up past an oil recycling collection point to come onto the village street of **Carrer de Levant**. We walk along the street, passing restored houses, to start climbing as we pass Nº18. A steady ascent brings us up to the level of the new villas as we go over the crest and stroll down to where the street turns sharp left. At this corner we go down onto the limestone slabs which form the top of the cliffs **(49.791N 17.857E)**.

Walking out across the slabs, we look back to see that the headland stands above a large cave. There are no marked paths across the limestone as we walk above more large sea caves to pass on the seaward side of a white house. Past the house, we walk around more 'discarded weetabix' limestone slabs, to go left and join the main walking trail. We pass more 'weetabix' as we stroll across still more unusual rock slabs to come onto the rather sanitised seafront of **S'Algar (49.992N 17.998E)**. Drinks and food are available around the seafront swimming pool, and our Walk 11, 'From The New To The Old' which finishes in **Binissaida**, starts here.

ALTERNATIVE RETURNS

If you are returning to **Punta Prima**, you can choose from our alternative routes to vary your journey.

1. The first option is to stay on the main walking trail from **S'Algar**, to pass on the inland side of the white house to come out onto the end of a cul-de-sac, **Carrer de Xaloc**. Going past **Piccollo Mundo**, the street turns left and comes onto **Alcalfar**'s 'main street'. We go right to walk past **Bar Via Maris** and the bus stop, where you'll find a plan of this little town. We could go left to join our outward route at this point.

2. Our second option is to continue down **Alcalfar**'s main street until it runs into a parking area behind the **Xuroy** apartments. Across the car park, we go left to walk out onto the large, gated bridge over the *barranco*. At the end of the bridge we step through a gap onto a walking trail which runs up alongside a substantial stone wall. In a few metres a path goes left which joins our outward route amongst the trees.

3. Our third option is to continue up the walking trail beside the wall. It's a steady climb as we toil up to the crest of the headland before taking the easy descent down to join our outward trail at the old well.

4. Our fourth and final option is to skip the diversion to the tower and take the main trail over the headland.

If you are walking to **S'Algar** and back on a warm day you'll find the 'mass tourism' hostelries of **Punta Prima** a welcome sight at the end of your return route!

10A. SHORT CUT TO WALK 11

If you are linking the coastal route of Walk 10 with the inland route of Walk 11, then it is not necessary to sample the delights of **S'Algar** along the way. Here is a short cut route from **Alcalfar** which links the two walks.

As we come to overlook **Cala d'Alcalfar** we could keep on the trail ahead instead of going down to the beach, to come onto the stone bridge and walk across to the car parking area behind the **Xuroy**. Walking up from the car park, we come onto **Alcalfar**'s main street and continue along it until we come to a public telephone, where we turn left to walk up **Carrer Tramuntana** (sign on the first house on the left). It's a steady climb on the tiled pavement, past small and large villas. Just before reaching the main road we go left on a little street, **Carrer de S'Ermita**, to walk along to a 'spaghetti western' church. At the church we go up to cross the main road **(49.921N 17.648E)** and walk away from **Alcalfar**. When we come to the impressive maroon presence of **San Pancracio** we continue to the end of its garden wall, to turn right onto a dirt lane **(49.982N 17.557E)**. As we walk down the lane past **San Pancracio**'s tennis court and vegetable plots, we can see the route of Walk 11, 'From The New To The Old', across the valley from us. The lane twists down into the small valley, and a gentle climb brings us up to cross the main road **(50.150N 17.648E)** into **S'Algar** and onto the route of Walk 11.

11. FROM THE NEW TO THE OLD

A delightful country route with an interesting diversion, using old country lanes and trails. Unfortunately, the start of a public right of way has been closed off by the riding school at the **S'Algar Country Club**, so the new route starts on country roads.

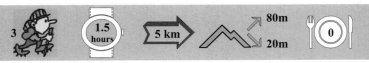

3 | 1.5 hours | 5 km | 80m / 20m | 0

We start out from **S'Algar** seafront by walking up the road behind the seafront pool bar, to join the **Sant Lluís** road at the roundabout. Continuing on the **Sant Lluís** road, we walk up to where a dirt road goes up through pine trees on our right **(50.150N 17.648E)**. Walk 10A, 'Short Cut To Walk 11' joins us from the dirt lane on the opposite side of the main road. We walk uphill under the pines to pass **C'an Domir** on our left. The lane continues gently uphill between a scattering of new and traditional houses to come up to a junction of trails **(50.316N 17.704E)**. On our right is the original route which now runs down to the country club and a second trail through the trees. To our left is an entrance which has been narrowed by stones to the width of a small rustic gate, once the route to an interesting diversion but unfortunately no longer accessible.

The lane levels out at the junction and then runs gently downhill, a lane going off to our right before we reach the end of vehicle navigation at a locked chain over a cattle grid. Taking care not to fall between the widely spaced bars, we cross the grid and step over the chain, to come into a woodland area. We follow the path past a 'fire warning' sign to walk alongside a high stone wall. The trail leads down into a valley, stone walls now marking the right of our trail as it curves around an old limestone cutting area. At the second gap in the stone wall is the start of our 11A, 'Cala des Rafalet' **(50.515N 17.742E)**. Our trail, now a limestone road, twists down past the old quarry to swing right onto a substantial stone bridge **(50.552N 17.714E)** which spans the valley. At the far side of the bridge we come to the best known of the trails down to **Cala des Rafalet**, and the signboard for **Barranco de Rafalet**.

The limestone road gets rougher as we climb up from the bridge to a small electricity pylon. We leave the road to go onto a walking trail on our left, to pass beneath the pylon and cross a stone wall. The path runs parallel to the stone wall across open countryside, and at the end of the wall we step through a pedestrian entrance to come back onto the lane in front of a chained entrance. Turning left, we stroll along the little-used lane with a shallow valley of neatly walled but abandoned fields on our right. We come along the lane to the imposing façade of **Rafalet Nou (50.776N 17.776E),** possibly the only traditional farmhouse on the island with a Greco-Roman extension!

At **Rafalet Nou** we go through rustic gates (not locked) to pass the house on our right as we continue on the limestone lane. It's an easy stroll along the lane between long-abandoned fields filled with thistles (or perhaps they farm thistles?). Gradually we approach the entrance gates of **Rafael Nou** to find them locked (this seems to be the normal situation) **(50.963N 17.505E)**. The easiest way past the gates is to use the *botadores* (wall steps) in the left hand wall and walk carefully along the wall to climb down outside the gates. We come onto a tarmac lane where Walk 12, 'A Stroll To Trebalúger' goes left, while we turn right for an easy stroll along to the end of the lane at the entrance to **Son Vidal (51.025N 17.660E)**.

At the entrance to **Son Vidal** we take the old donkey trail, part of **Camí de Cavalls**, which is on our left. This final section to reach **Binissaida** is a 'rescued by pruning' route; in June 96 we re-opened this old trail at the cost of two pairs of secateurs and very blistered hands, so do expect to push past plants and bushes. If you could also do your share of pruning along this section

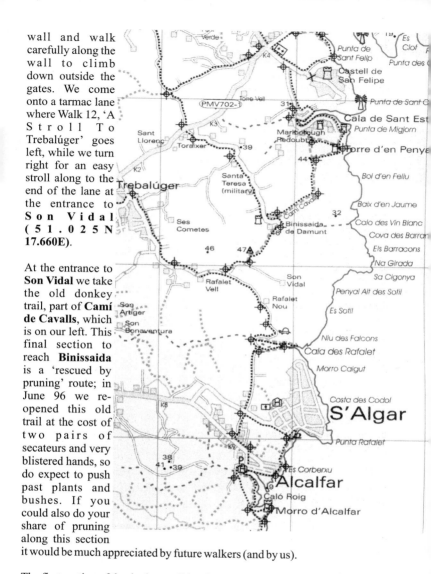

it would be much appreciated by future walkers (and by us).

The first section of the donkey trail is relatively clear, but where the trail turns right the serious plant growth begins. It is a case of pushing through and cutting back plants and bushes, with no views to either side or ahead for about five minutes until we come to the back of one of the traditional farmhouses. From this point the route becomes clearer, making it a lot easier to emerge from the **Camí de Cavalls** (complete with sign) onto the end of a tarmac lane **(51.260N 17.895E)**. We follow the lane left, ignoring any dirt roads, to come around the farmhouse to its entrance where the lane turns right. The lane now goes past the classical 'fortified' farmhouse of **Binissaida**, although due to the high stone walls we can only enjoy a partial view of this classic structure from its entrance drive. From the traditional farmhouses, we stroll down between much newer weekender smallholdings, many with noisy guard dogs, to pass a sign, 'Hort de Lavi 29, 29A, 34', set in the right hand wall. Just a few metres on, we come to the end of our route with the **Horts de Binissaida** street sign at a junction where we join the route of Walk 4, 'Escape From The Tower', coming along the lane from the right.

11A. CALA DES RAFALET

Cala des Rafalet is one of Menorca's most beautiful inlets, thought by many to be accessible only by boat. In fact, there are at least two paths which lead to this hidden inlet.

Our preferred route is to leave the limestone road at the second gap in the stone wall, to come onto a narrow walking trail. The trail goes down across a wild meadow towards trees, where we come onto natural limestone steps. We follow the trail as it threads its way round the edge of the trees to go through a substantial stone wall. Coming into another meadow, we go gently uphill to cross limestone slabs and come to a split in the trail.

We take the left hand trail and come through a gap in a stone wall (take care here) to step down into a green wood. The narrow path twists it way down through the trees and comes down to stone steps. From the steps, we carefully walk down a stone wall to dive into the darker wood. We drop down to a picnic area beneath the trees at the head of the inlet **(50.544N 17.921E)**, and down a little further is a tiny beach, which we cross to come onto rocks running along the inlet. Taking care on the rocks, we go a little way along the inlet in order to appreciate its beauty, and as we make our way along we come to a garage (!) built in this unlikely and inaccessible location. Returning from **Cala des Rafalet**, we can take a variation by walking up through the picnic area to follow the main trail up to the stone bridge.

12. A STROLL TO TREBALÚGER

A gentle country stroll on quiet lanes which links Walk 11, 'From The New To The Old' with the archaeological site of Trebalúger, as an alternative to the **Camí de Cavalls** route to **Binissaida**.

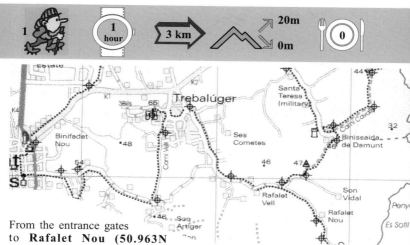

From the entrance gates to **Rafalet Nou (50.963N 17.505E)**, we go left to stroll along the lane beneath an avenue of pines which give welcome shade on hot days. The flat tarmac lane makes for relaxed walking as our route winds between fields, mostly fallow but with a pungent pig field just before we pass the entrance to **Rafalet Vell (50.965N 17.266E)**. We come along to a mixture of piggeries and stables as the lane narrows and the roofs of houses on the outskirts of **Trebalúger** come into sight. The narrow lane twists and weaves between the fields, passing the 'fortified' farmhouse of **Rafalet Petit** on our left. We pass a lane **(51.090N 17.002E)** which runs past **Pou Nou** into **Sant Lluís**; further on, this lane forms part of Walk 13, 'New Well And Refreshments'. Just before reaching the village of **Trebalúger**, the remains of a cottage contrast with the affluent houses just ahead of us. Passing the entrance to Nº74, we stroll between the large, modern houses with cul-de-sacs going off both sides of the lane.

We stay on the main lane, **Camí de Rafalet**, winding our way through this prosperous village until we reach house Nº34 on our left **(51.412N 16.779E)**. **Camí de Rafalet** goes right towards the main road as we go onto **Carrer de San Torre**. This little lane runs between high stone walls to come to the **Camí des Pou**. We turn right into the tiny lane, to pass a 'fortified' farmhouse and go straight on past **Camí de Garofer**. At the house, **Trebalúger Nova**, we swing right to walk down to a junction signed to the **Talaiot de Trebalúger (51.414N 16.636E)**.

We head along the tiny lane towards the *talaiot*'s stone mound, passing **Can Lavi** and some abandoned farm buildings as we come up to the archaeological site entrance. A path leads into the site and straight up to the summit of the *talaiot* **(51.411N 16.521E)**. The best views are gained by standing on the stones in the centre of the circle, from where we can look out over the flat plateau of the region.

13. NEW WELL AND REFRESHMENTS

In common with other archaeological sites, **Trebalúger** has a distinct lack of refreshments. The logical place to head for is the small town of **Sant Lluís**. To reach the town, we take a very countrified route on a mixture of donkey trail and country lanes, along with a short diversion through the traditional farming village of **Pou Nou** (New Well).

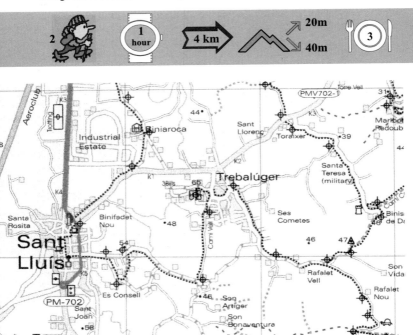

From the **Trebalúger** *talaiot* (**51.411N 16.521E**), we retrace the route of Walk 12, 'A Stroll To Trebalúger', back to the house **Trebalúger Nova**. Here, Walk 11 comes in from the left on **Camí des Pou**, and this time we turn right to follow the little lane between new villas to a cross-roads with the **Carrer Ametllers**. We come onto a new street development complete with concrete seats where we go to our front right, skirting the edge of the village to come out onto a very narrow lane. This dirt lane runs down past **Las Ruedas** (a house) and a junction with another dirt lane (**51.253N 16.585E**). We go straight ahead on **Camí Vell**. The lane runs down between stone walls to open out at the large entrance to house Nº20. At the next house, **Sa Lavi** on the left, the lane ceases to be used for vehicle access and narrows down to a stone-laid donkey trail.

It is gently downhill past a modern farm building on our right as the trail runs a little above the countryside, giving us views over the shallow, fallow valley on our left. We continue down the lumpy trail, passing a donkey trail on our right which is completely filled with pistacia bushes. After a narrow waist-like section our trail widens out and starts to run gently uphill, passing an impressive gated entrance on our left. We come up alongside large tubular greenhouses to join a tarmac lane (the same lane that features in Walk 11, 'From The New To The Old' and in Walk 12, 'A Stroll To Trebalúger', from the **Rafalet Nou** entrance) **(50.879N 16.532E)**.

Turning right, we stroll past the greenhouses on the smooth tarmac, and in contrast to the abandoned fields alongside the donkey trail, this is an area of intensively farmed weekender small holdings. A little further along, a small lane runs off left to **Casas Vells** (the sign is very worn) as we come up to a pair of modern houses on the outskirts of **Pou Nou**. In the right hand house the guard dog even has his own Carlsberg sun umbrella.

Just past the houses, a tiny lane is signed to **Es Pou Nou (51.024N 15.969E)**, and here we take an interesting diversion off the direct route to **Sant Lluís**. Going down the narrow lane, we pass an old farmhouse as our route snakes along between the old houses of the village, a direct contrast to the manufactured opulence of **Trebalúger**. We come down into a shallow valley to pass the well that gives the village its name. The lane squeezes up between traditional houses and farm buildings, to swing right and left around houses before we come to a junction **(50.882N 15.928E)**. The spire of the **Sant Lluís** church is ahead of us as we turn right on the 'main' lane. We leave the village centre behind as we stroll past cultivated fields to rejoin the tarmac lane **(51.022N 15.852E)**, an **Es Pou Nou** sign pointing back the way we have come.

We turn left on the lane to go gently uphill between houses, a tiny lane joining us from the left. Passing an old house with a 'Madonna and Child' statue set in its wall, we come to the outskirts of **Sant Lluís**. At the main road **(51.036N 15.664E)** we cross straight over onto **Carrer de Sant Antoni** to meet the town's main street alongside the church at the second junction. Here we have a choice of *tipico* bars for refreshments; the air-conditioned luxury of **La Rueda** is the furthest bar along the street on our right.

14. AN HISTORICAL TOUR

Don't be disappointed by the urban industrial landscape at the start of this walk; just wait for the dramatic change when we step out into the countryside on our 'Historical Tour'. For once hire-car drivers are well catered for, as the route can be made circular by using the outer road of the industrial estate, while 'true' walkers will appreciate the urban/rural contrast which comes from starting in **Maó**.

3 | 2 hours | 8 km | 70m / 70m | 3

Our starting point is by the underground car park in **Plaça Esplanada (53.340N 15.619E)** which we leave by walking up **Carrer Vassallo**. It is a steady uphill pavement stroll, passing the English Bookshop for us to come to the roundabout on **Avinguda Vives Llull (53.298N 15.385E)**. We go straight over the roundabout on the **Carrer Vassallo** to leave the old city behind, and come into the modern commercial suburbs. Past the dun-coloured school, the athletic stadium adds a splash of colour in this rather bleak environment. At the next roundabout **(53.216N 15.106E)** (part of the town's ring road) we meet the edge of the industrial estate and leave the main road (no pavement) to walk along the quieter arterial road (with pavement) which parallels it. **Maó**'s industrial suburb does have some splashes of colour, although on this section we could be on a warehouse estate anywhere in Spain. It is easy walking along the perimeter of the estate to reach its furthest point, two kilometres from **Plaça Esplanada (52.949N 14.272E)**.

At the end of the estate we go right to walk down between warehouses until we come to a **Centro de Protección de Animales** sign at the entrance to a lane **(53.033N 14.239E)**. Leaving the tarmac, we go down the lane which swings left in front of the entrance lane to the dog pound. Ahead is a very different vista of bucolic rural charm, as we follow the lane up through a limestone cutting behind a smelly factory, to run out below an impressive outcrop. The lane continues below the outcrop, on towards the old farmhouse of **Curnia Vell**, while we go left onto a limestone donkey trail. It's gently uphill as the trail narrows to a walking path between old stone walls with bushes pushing in on our route. The bushes give way and the walls become lower to give us views across to the old farmhouse of **Curnia Nou** on our right, as the trail runs onto a dirt lane. Industry is not quite left behind, as we pass a large former quarrying area where some of the excavated caves have become large garages, and head towards **Maó**'s car scrapyard.

At the entrance to **Ternia Nou (52.947N 13.943E)** a tarmac lane comes in from the left. We continue straight ahead on a rough stone lane, passing the scrap-yard and an electricity sub-station on our right as we climb up to **Villa Francisco** - a traditional white farmhouse. Another fifty metres brings us up to a busy main road **(52.944N 13.764E)** which we cross with care, going straight over onto a small dirt lane which runs into the small village of **Ses Casetes Noves** (not signed). Following the lane, we pass a scruffy yard with noisy (chained) guard dogs on our right, as we head between the few houses. The lane becomes less used after house Nº25, then becoming unused past the next house (with a 'witch' weathervane). We walk along the overgrown track to come to a traditional *camino real* donkey trail. This is another of our 'rescued by pruning' donkey trails where we spent some time with secateurs re-establishing the trail. Be prepared to push through some foliage, and please bend back or prune the bushes and brambles. Keeping this route open is important, as the alternative route involves walking along busy main roads without pavements.

The start of the *camino* is relatively clear as we walk down between high stone walls. Brambles become prominent (please prune) for fifty metres, before the trail goes right by a field entrance. We go gently downhill through a leisurely S-bend, an old farmstead on our left. Our trail runs down to mature trees on the right of the path which clothe the remains of a hut, before running along to join a lane below a traditional white farmhouse **(52.800N 13.532E)**. The stony lane climbs up to reach a crest with a house and a barn on our left, before running downhill towards the airport landing lights. A small rise brings the lane up to join a tarmac lane under the array of landing lights **(52.736N 13.396E)**.

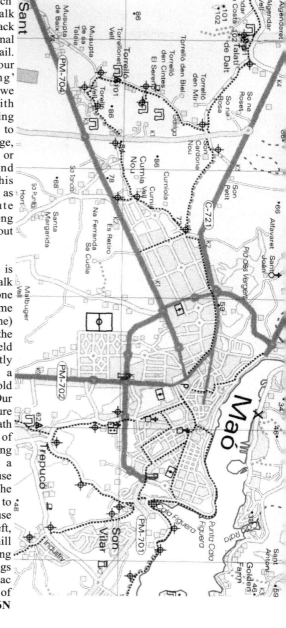

We turn right and in a few metres take the narrow dirt lane **(52.820N 13.275E)** signed to **El Sereno** restaurant. The narrow dirt lane runs gently uphill between stone walls to go across the landing lights, and weaves its way through the countryside. At another sign for **El Sereno** we pass a lane off on our left as we come in sight of the **Torrelló** *talaiot*, unusual for the window on its summit. From our viewpoint, the *talaiot* also appears to have a modern chimney! Another 100 metres brings us up to one of Menorca's largest *talaiots* and its unusual entrance **(52.924N 13.313E)**. The **Torrelló** *talaiot* is contained within a high stone wall with a narrow flight of traditional wall steps or *botadores*, to climb onto the wall by the signboard. From the top of the wall there is an even more precipitous flight of steps into the compound. The descent, and the climb back out, along with traversing the compound, calls for a high level of agility, and if you have any doubts on this score, we would advise you not to go down the narrow steps. Also within the compound are some well shafts covered with discarded pallets, and many of the stones are less secure than they appear - altogether a less friendly archaeological site than most!

From the *talaiot* we continue down the lane; note that the entrance to **Torellonet Vell**, passing between farmhouses and fields, is private. As the lane levels out past the houses, we see an unusual modern structure away on our right. A couple of minutes brings us to the junction of **Fornas de Torrelló (53.189N 13.435E)**. Leaving the main lane, we stroll along to the basilica mosaic that is housed below a modern roof. Once the floor of an early Christian church (6th century AD), the repeated bird patterns are well preserved. Unfortunately, the chain-link fencing and opaque perspex which protects the area prevents the taking of good photographs from the elevated viewing walkway.

We walk down from the mosaic to rejoin the lane and turn right towards **El Serrano** (The Ham), and a gentle downhill stroll brings us down to the restaurant, only open from 20.00-23.00 hours and from May to October! Our trail continues gently uphill, passing a villa on our left as the lane becomes rougher underfoot, then running along between two unnamed old farmhouses. We see good specimens of 'bears' breeches' (Acanthus) on the left of the lane as we leave the farmhouses behind and sneak off downhill past a new villa, also unnamed. It is gently downhill despite the lane's rough surface, getting rougher as it gets steeper. We come down towards street lights to the junction of dirt lanes which is the start of Walk 15, 'More Historical Sights' **(53.439N 13.682E)**.

Walk 15 goes left while we follow a **Maó, Ciutadella** sign nailed to a wall to go under the main road. Emerging from the tunnel, the lane undulates along to another junction **(53.488N 13.851E)**, where a **Maó, Ciutadella** sign points left towards the C-721 **Maó-Alaior** main road. Ignoring the sign, we walk along the dirt lane, paralleling the C-721, to pass **Son Cardona Nou** on our right. Our route undulates along through the countryside, the stone walls high on one section, passing the electricity distribution transformers on our left before curving round a large spinney. The lane starts descending gently towards the industrial estate to emerge onto the perimeter road by a car storage depot **(53.347N 14.495E)**. Car drivers should follow the perimeter road for approximately 400 metres to where our outward route went into the countryside, to pick up their hire car. Walkers will find it easiest to go over onto **Calle 6** and cut through the estate to rejoin our outward route for the return into **Maó**.

15. MORE HISTORICAL SIGHTS

This walk follows a mixture of country lanes linking an important *talaiot* and *taula* site with the best preserved *navetas* on the island. Much of the walking is on narrow tarmac lanes, although the start is on a much rougher 'four wheel drive' track.

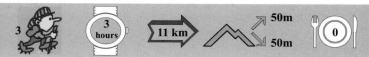

Our starting point is the country lane which leaves the route of Walk 14, 'An Historical Tour' as it turns back towards **Maó (53.439N 13.682E)**. If you are tackling Walk 15 as a separate walk from **Maó**, then follow Walk 14 to **Calle 6** on the industrial estate. Down **Calle 6** and across the perimeter road, we come onto Walk 14's return route, a dirt lane. Follow this lane to its second junction with a **Maó, Ciutadella** sign to reach the start of Walk 15. If you have used these directions to access the start, then add an hour to the time shown on the key.

We start out along the rough country lane which parallels the C-721 **Maó-Alaior** road. Our route runs through wild abandoned countryside, climbing gently past field entrances on our left. Blackberries are taking over the stone walls, and the lane's surface becomes solid limestone, not always flat, before resuming its rough surface to run downhill between stone walls to a pair of field entrances. The views over the fields, mostly of thistle, improve as we walk along towards a radio transmitter mast. We climb gently on limestone slabs and laid boulders up to a crest between a large limestone outcrop and the radio mast, to come out on a tarmac lane **(53.696N 13.121E)**. Fifty metres to our left is the purple sign at the entrance to **Talatí de Dalt**.

To reach the archaeological site we cross a stepped wall and follow a grass and boulder track up to the site entrance **(53.661N 12.978E)**. Going clockwise round the rock mound, we come to the unusual standing stone which makes the site unique. A sloping stone is set to support the 'T' piece - or could it be part of a stone ring which has slowly toppled over three millennia? It is an easy climb to the top of the stone mound from where we enjoy views over the countryside and away to the **Ermita Mare de Deu del Toro** on Menorca's only mountain. This site, along with most other *talaiot* sites, gives the impression of having been only cursorily investigated, supported by the large cave hidden by a tree near the site entrance.

From **Talatí de Dalt** we continue along the narrow tarmac lane **(W)** with views across to the restored farmhouse and buildings of **Algendaret** set in a limestone outcrop. Our route wriggles around an outcrop of limestone to come past excellent specimens of wild flowers and to an electricity sub-station. The lane swings left and climbs gently up alongside **Algendar Vell**. Over the crest of the rise, we pass a dirt lane on our left, followed by another restored farmhouse as we stroll gently downhill. Blackberry brambles and bushes restrict our views as the lane twists between stone walls and past a patch of wild dog roses to come to a woodland area. Ahead is a square tower, our lane gently rising to come up to the electricity sub-station on a junction of

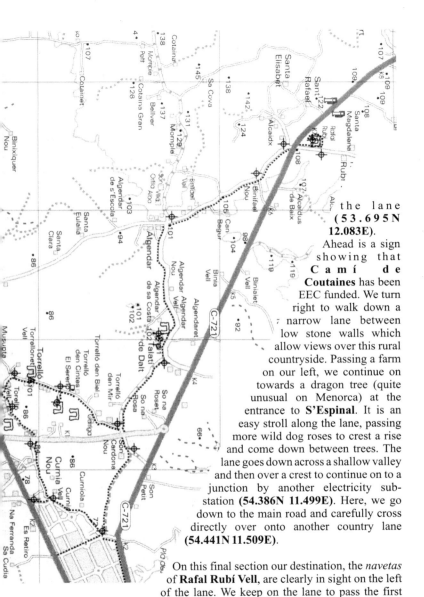

the lane (**53.695N 12.083E**).

Ahead is a sign showing that **Camí de Coutaines** has been EEC funded. We turn right to walk down a narrow lane between low stone walls which allow views over this rural countryside. Passing a farm on our left, we continue on towards a dragon tree (quite unusual on Menorca) at the entrance to **S'Espinal**. It is an easy stroll along the lane, passing more wild dog roses to crest a rise and come down between trees. The lane goes down across a shallow valley and then over a crest to continue on to a junction by another electricity sub-station (**54.386N 11.499E**). Here, we go down to the main road and carefully cross directly over onto another country lane (**54.441N 11.509E**).

On this final section our destination, the *navetas* of **Rafal Rubí Vell**, are clearly in sight on the left of the lane. We keep on the lane to pass the first *naveta*, following the land owner's signs along to a rustic gate entrance. Through the gate, we come onto a small path which runs along the edge of a cornfield to the first of the *hypostyle* chambers, a well-preserved example that you can crawl into, its stone-slab roof supported on pillars. The path continues into another field where we find the larger of the *navetas*, a boat-shaped burial chamber constructed from limestone boulders. In common with the other archaeological sites, there are no refreshments to be had here, the nearest possibility being the CEPSA service station shops, another two hundred metres along the main road. Our return is back along our outward route, making a long country walk through the beautiful, tranquil rural landscape.

16. CALA DEL PILAR

Menorca has many beautiful beaches and bays, and **Cala del Pilar** is up there with the best of them. This walk takes us to a beautiful, unspoilt 'castaway' style bay. Just remember to take swim wear and a picnic to make the most of it.

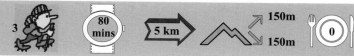

3 | 80 mins | 5 km | 150m / 150m | 0

We park at the grassed area alongside the dirt road **(02.229N 58.438E)** and stroll down the few metres to the start of the walk at a gap in the stone wall **(02.257N 58.440E)**. Keeping to the main track, we head up a sandy path through the holm oaks in a steady ascent **(NE)**.

Our gradient moderates **(5M)** as our route swings left **(02.342N 58.560E, N)**, and then the path changes from hard dirt to soft sand for the next climb **(02.390N 58.528E)**. The path levels out and reverts to hard dirt **(02.452N 58.512E, 9M, alt. 300 ft/91m)** to overlook the valley on our left as we start to climb again **(02.601N 58.517E, 323ft/98m, N)** and then swings right **(02.669N 58.575E, 328ft/100m, 15M)** before starting to run downhill.

Pines have now replaced the oaks alongside the path as we come down to a fallen tree by a path to the left **(02.733N 58.584E)**. We continue downhill in a gully until the water runoff goes

down to our right **(02.806N 58.611E)**, for us to continue on a smooth woodland path, walking beneath green boughs. Emerging from the trees **(21M)**, we come amongst sand dunes to continue downhill **(N)**, and the sea comes into view **(23M)**.

We come down to the edge of the cliffs **(02.988N 58.652E)** where a walking trail climbs up from the beach, our preferred return route, before continuing down between dunes **(03.018N 58.734E, 27M)** to an area of red mud on our left **(03.074N 58.830E)**. Keeping to the left hand gully, we drop steadily down to the soft sand beach with its convenient bleached tree trunks ideal for sitting on **(03.118N 58.745E)** - but watch out for the ants. Here you can relax on one of the least visited Menorcan coves, or stroll across the sand to the stone beach house **(40M)**.

After enjoying this five star bay, we return from the centre of the beach **(03.093N 58.690E)**, following the clear track up to the base of the slope. Above us and on our left, a pair of substantial cave houses can be seen built in the top of the cliff as we struggle uphill through he soft sand. We come onto rock for an easier though still energetic climb up towards the cutting in the top of the cliffs.

Once on top of the cliffs, our outward route lies to our left but we go right, climbing up a dirt path to reach a crest **(02.962N 58.598E)**. We keep to the main path as a small track goes right **(02.945N 58.574E)** to continue steadily up through the trees. Our path comes alongside a stone wall until the two diverge **(02.809N 58.565E)** and we climb gently up until we swing left to drop down to the fallen tree **(02.733N 58.584E)** of our outward route.

Now we retrace our steps through the wood and back to the car **(80M)**. There is only one thing missing from this straightforward walk to an exciting destination - a *tipico*. As it is several kilometres to the nearest refreshment, don't forget to bring a picnic!

17. CALA PREGONDA

Cala Pregonda is one of Menorca's most beautiful beaches, but public access has become restricted as landowners close off country roads. Our walking route offers the only open public access to this desirable destination.

3   50 mins   4 km   80m 80m   3

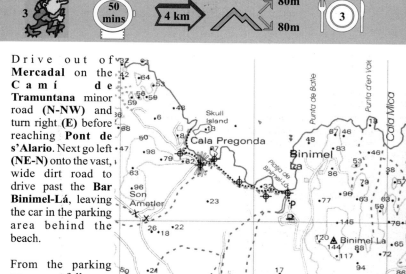

Drive out of **Mercadal** on the **Camí de Tramuntana** minor road (**N-NW**) and turn right (**E**) before reaching **Pont de s'Alario**. Next go left (**NE-N**) onto the vast, wide dirt road to drive past the **Bar Binimel-Lá**, leaving the car in the parking area behind the beach.

From the parking area, we follow a path, passing the lagoon on our left to come onto the beach from where we head west (**03.169N 03.259E, W**). At the end of the beach (**03.167N 03.186E**), we take the inland path to come up to a crude gate (**03.144N 03.097E**). Stepping through the gate, we walk down and pass the next beach (**03.190N 03.006E**) and a dirt road which goes off to our left, as we climb a red earth slope inland of cliffs. At the top of the climb we go through a wall, and **Cala Pregonda** comes into view.

Our trail heads **NW** through green dunes, and **Cala Pregonda** comes back into view as we top a dune and then drop down towards the beach (**03.338N 02.705E, 17M**). Past the beach, we climb up on red rock (**03.319N 02.665E**) and head for an electricity post, a steepish climb which brings us up to a gate onto the dirt road near the post (**03.349N 02.615E, 20M**). We now have an easy stroll along the dirt road, accompanied by panoramic views over the bay and **Skull Island**. The road drops down towards the bay where we take a path signed '*a la playa*' (**03.409N 02.487E**) and drop down through the bushes onto this immaculate beach. Take time to stroll along the beach and take advantage of this beautiful landscape while enjoying a swim and picnic.

We return by retracing our outward route. After the stiff climb up to the gate at the peak of the road, the return trip seems quite gentle!

18. TORRE DE SA NITJA - HISTORIC SURPRISES

For historic content, this walk is hard to beat, with relics from three different periods of Menorca's history. Equally surprising is that this route has never appeared on a map until now.

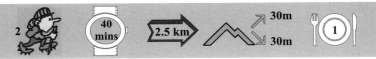

2 · 40 mins · 2.5 km · 30m / 30m · 1

From the **Santa Teresa Museum** car park **(04.014N 05.377E)**, a trail leads quite steeply down **(NNW)** to cross the lane **(SW)** and continue down into a small valley, to join a dirt road **(04.067N 05.352E, 5M)**. We go through a gate **(W)** to a junction of paths where we head north **(N)** along the line of the valley. Our route curves left past the head of **Port de Sanitja**, for us to go through a wall **(04.157N 05.314E)** for a short climb **(NNW)** to another gap in a wall alongside the excavated remains of a Roman villa, the shapes and sizes of the individual rooms still clearly visible **(04.220N 05.300E)**.

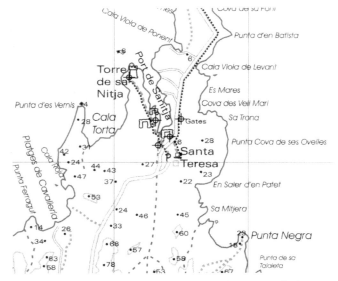

On through the wall, and in the next field we find an unusually long, partly overgrown *naveta*. We climb a small rise and the **Torre de sa Nitja** comes into view, and we pass through another wall **(04.288N 05.233E)** for our stony path to head directly towards the old tower **(04.469N 05.104E)**. We reach the tower in twenty minutes from the car park **(20M)**.

Unlike many of the coastal towers which can be viewed only from the outside, you can examine both the upper and lower floors of **Torre de sa Nitja**, though both are now used for shelter by the free-ranging sheep and goats! We return by retracing our outward route.

19. CAP DE CAVALLERIA

Although you can drive onto the **Cap de Cavalleria** peninsula on a good tarmac lane, walking this easy route to Menorca's northern point is much more enjoyable.

We drive out on the **Camí Cavelleria** as far as the museum at **Santa Teresa** and turn into its car park. You can buy simple refreshments from the museum's bar before setting off from beneath the shady trees on a path (**N**) which slopes gently down to the remains of a Roman village which straddles the tarmac lane (**04.111N 05.443E**).

From the village, we stroll along the tarmac lane with its views over the **Port de Sanitja** inlet to **Torre de Nitja** to a pair of wooden gates (**04.233N 05.481E**); please close these after you. It's easy strolling past dirt roads which lead down to small bays on our left (**W**), until the lane swings left (**NW**) to start climbing onto the plateau at the end of the peninsula, though this hardly counts as an energetic climb.

When the lane swings back to the north (**N**) by an old information point, we are back to easy strolling. A cliff-top ridge develops on our right as we walk towards the parking area (**05.316N 05.596E**) before the light house, some fifty minutes (**50M**) from **Santa Teresa**. Walking past the parking area, we take paths west (**W**) of the light house to come to old gun emplacements (**05.389N 05.503E**) at the top of the cliffs. We keep circling left to complete a circuit of the coastal battery and then follow a path (**E**) back to the parking area.

A tract-less mix of rock slabs and low scrub lies east of the lane, but crossing this is most rewarding. Aim for the low point in the cliff's ridge (**05.295N 05.650E**) and take care as you look over and down on the spectacular views of cliffs and churning sea.

We retrace our steps along the lane, mostly downhill this time, then up the path for celebratory drinks back beneath the shady trees.

20. PLAYA SON PARC TO THE HOUSE WITH NO NAME

The safe, soft white beach of **Son Parc** on Menorca's north coast makes a good starting point for this walk of scenic views, bays, beaches and a little history for good measure.

We begin at the bar/restaurant on the beach at **Son Parc (02.039N 09.666E)**. We walk across the beach through a gap in the stone wall, to follow the stony path **(N)** gently upwards alongside the azure waters of the bay towards a stone wall in the distance.

Through the second wall **(02.267N 09.671E)**, our stony path meanders uphill to a junction **(02.352N 09.720E, 14M)**. Taking the right path, the sea comes back into view and we come to an old gun emplacement **(02.393N 09.755E, 15M)**, from where we enjoy excellent views back into the bay of **Son Parc**. Stepping a few metres left, we join the second path to follow its route (still stony) over a small rise, which brings the 'house with no name' into view in the distance at the end of the headland. We drop down into a shallow valley and beach **(02.537N 09.655E, 20 M)**. Past the littered beach, we follow the brown path **(NW)** to climb gently before dropping down to overlook the cute bay of **Cala Pudent (02.657N 09.594E)**.

Our route swings left **(26M)** for us to walk gently up and away from **Cala Pudent** and then levels out to head **WSW (02.582N 09.410E, 30M)** as our path widens to vehicle width heading west **(W)**. Now pine trees accompany the pistacia and cistus bushes which grow taller here than on the exposed coast earlier on our route, as we follow the broad track along **(SSW)** to a junction with a main dirt road **(02.345N 09.019E, 40M)**.

Now we swing right **(N-NNW)** to face the old house at the head of the peninsula. We have a choice of three dirt roads, all heading in the same general direction and coming together later on at a particularly large pine tree **(02.695N 08.921E, 49M)**. Our easy stroll becomes slightly more difficult as the abandoned house of **S'Albufereta** comes into view, and our track becomes stony as it rises up the gentle slope. Old grey stone walls peep out of the bushes, lending a tired and abandoned air to the landscape as we approach the ruined house.

Passing the house entrance **(02.975N 08.881E, 55M)**, we walk up the stony track **(N)** to the edge of a valley. The stony road swings right **(03.167N 08.829E)** as we go straight down a very stony track heading for the sea. Ahead, the continuation of the stony track is clearly visible as it climbs the slopes up to the old houses. It is a skittery descent alongside an old stone wall before we come alongside a tiny inlet with a white sand beach **(13.390N 08.688E, 67M)**. Over a small ridge and past a second inlet with its own landing stage **(03.491N 08.557E, 72M)**, we start to climb quite seriously. Sunglasses are recommended in sunny weather, to help reduce the reflected

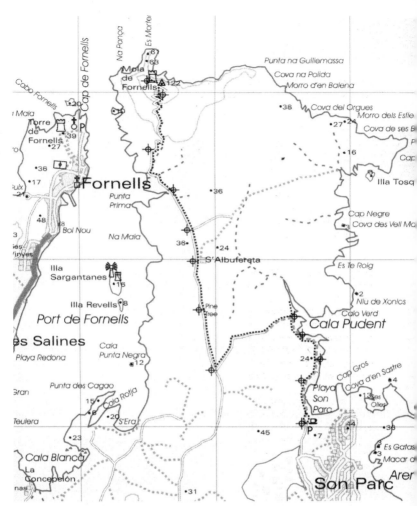

glare from the light stone surface as we toil up the relentless slopes. It is steadily upwards alongside a bush-filled valley on a straight ascent, before the road starts to zigzag (**03.633N 08.548E, 75M**). The gradient now eases for an easy walk past rosemary bushes, steadily ascending until at the final zigzags (**03.868N 08.602E, 88M**) we take a path to short-cut the road. Past a cave and stone quarry on our right, we cross the road onto another path (**N**) before rejoining the road for the last bend up to the first house (**03.941N 08.599E**). This is not an old farm, but a military officers' house, and we turn left to cross the open ground and pass the barracks building to come up onto the gun positions (**04.038N 08.618E, 100M**) above the cliffs at the head of the peninsula. A look-out point gives spectacular cliff views as we enjoy this most isolated of Menorcan destinations.

We return by the same route, to arrive for refreshments on the bar terrace overlooking **Son Parc** beach, approximately **3.5 hours** since we passed it on our outward journey.

21. CAP DE FAVARITX

Many visitors get to **Cap de Favaritx** but only explore the immediate area. Follow our walk and you'll be rewarded by deserted beaches and a bird-watcher's paradise. Remember to take along a picnic, as you will be a long way from refreshments.

3 | 1.5 hours | 4.5 km | 170m / 170m | 0

We start at **Cap de Favaritx** after driving along the country lane and parking alongside the road, quite busy at weekends but often deserted on weekdays.

We walk around the rustic gates **(59.871N 15.473E)** to come onto a broad stony track which heads through the slate landscape, climbing gently and gradually curving **(SW-W)** amongst the stone, shrub-clothed dunes **(59.701N 15.317E, 10M)**. We come to a junction **(59.669N 15.242E, 12M)** where a rough track continues ahead as we swing left on the dirt road **(S)** to come onto a rise overlooking **Cala Presili**, with Menorca's eastern coastline disappearing into the misty distance. Now it is gently down through zigzags (short cuts are possible) to the end of the road above the beach **(59.615N 15.329E, 15M)**.

Paths take us down to **Cala Presili** where polished slate and pebbles line this small beach at the mouth of the valley. From the southern end of the beach we can either take a path which climbs steadily up the northern side of a small valley, or the steeper ascent over open ground (on a faint path) onto the headland **(59.497N 15.325E, 23M)** to look down on the beautiful and probably deserted beach of **Platja de Capifort**. Inland from the beach are the **Aveagua** wetlands where bird watchers should seek a comfortable vantage point amongst the high dunes.

A variety of paths take us slip sliding down through the high dunes **(S)**, or we can take a cliff-side path down to an old wall **(59.437N 15.353E)** to come onto the impressive beach **(30M)**. It is easiest to follow a route alongside the lagoon's vegetation to reach the end of the beach **(59.342N 15.395E)**, where

we take a small path which climbs up the headland. After 50 metres we have a choice of routes **(59.330N 15.413E)**, either straight up or continuing on the main path for a gentler ascent. Once on the top, we continue **SE** to overlook a small bay as we head down to an old wall. Through the wall **(59.282N 15.493E, 28M)**, we gently ascend **(E/SE)** to the top of the cliffs **(59.264N 15.616E, 43M)** and stroll along to a small plateau on **Cap de Ses Piques**, overlooking **Cala Morella Nou (45M)**, a beautiful, isolated spot from which to enjoy the tranquil side of Menorca. To return, we retrace our steps.

22. ES GRAU PENINSULA

The **Es Grau** peninsula area has much to offer in addition to its beach, village and waterside bars and restaurants. Our first walk in this area takes us along an idyllic coastline with pocket-sized beaches.

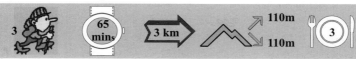

We start from the car park at the entrance to **Es Grau (57.015N 16.106E)** to walk around the beach and onto a broad dirt and rock path **(57.233N 15.924E)** which climbs up onto the headland. We pass a path **(57.284N 16.005E)** and over a saddle to come into the next valley, where we pass a path **(57.309N 15.978E)** which drops to the valley floor. Passing another path off to our right **(57.346N 15.974E)**, we come amongst trees **(14M)** to pass through a stone wall **(57.365N 15.908E)** on a gradual ascent up the wooded slope. At **15M** a small path goes off to our left **(57.375N 15.842E)** as we stay on the main path, curving up through the trees **(NNW)**. We come out of the tree to a track junction **(57.402N 15.876E)** and then on to a gap in a stone wall **(57.421N 15.943E, 20M)**, the path narrowing as it reaches the high point of this section of the route.

Now it is gently down **(E)** past a path off to the right **(57.443N 16.058E)**, and we lose the views of **Es Grau** before a gentle rise brings the village back into view, and our path heads towards **Es Grau**. At a T-junction **(57.369N 16.134E)** we go left **(ENE, 24M)** and left again at another fork **(57.379N 16.155E)** to head towards **Illa d'en Colom (ENE)**. A stony path **(57.404N 16.203E)** takes us down towards a tiny beach, and we then stroll along above azure waters, passing below a cave house before passing through a wall **(57.481N 16.206E)**. After a short drop our stony path angles away from the straights **(57.536N 16.224E)** and past the last of the tiny beaches which face **Illa d'en Colom** to bring us up onto the rocky headland **(32M)**.

The headland is a trackless area, so we take our direction towards an old tower **(57.632N 16.126E)** before curving **(SW)** towards a sandy beach to come onto

a discernible path **(57.597N 16.036E)**. We come alongside an inlet **(S)** to swing right across its head **(57.535N 15.987E)** and then over a saddle to go down the narrow path **(57.544N 15.922E)** with pampas-like grasses and pistacia bushes pushing in on our route before we reach the beach. It's a good idea to take a break on this quiet beach before tackling our return route. From the end of the beach, we head inland on a small rough path which soon climbs intensely.

It is a stiff climb up the valley to meet our outward route once more **(57.375N 15.842E, 50M)**. We retrace our outward route, the waterside bars of **Es Grau** proving a powerful magnet to guide us back to base **(65M)**.

23. TORRE BLANCA

Menorca is rich in archaeological sites, but **Torre Blanca** is one of the most interesting, perhaps made more so because it has not been 'manicured'. Add to this a varied route taking in coastline and country meadows for a great value walk. Refreshments are available only at the start and end of this walk, so take food and drink with you.

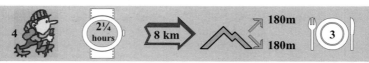

We start from the car park at the entrance to **Es Grau (57.015N 16.106E)** to walk around the beach and onto a broad dirt and rock path **(57.233N 15.924E)** which climbs up onto the headland. We pass a path **(57.284N 16.005E)** and over a saddle to come into the next valley, where we pass a path **(57.309N 15.978E)** which drops to the valley floor. Passing another path off to our right **(57.346N 15.974E)**, we come amongst trees **(14M)** to pass through a stone wall **(57.365N 15.908E)** on a gradual ascent up the wooded slope.

At **15M** we go left on a small path **(57.375N 15.842E)** while the main path continues curving up through the trees. We come out of the foliage to look down on the idyllic bay of **Fondeadero de los Llanes**. A narrow, steep path drops us down the sharp valley before running out to join a coastal path at the end of the beach **(57.536N 15.897E, 20M)**. We cross the beach to climb up **(NW)** to a gap in the wall **(57.590N 15.814E)**. We then drop down the left path which brings us onto a dirt road **(57.616N 15.789E)**. Going right, we have an easy stroll along the dirt road and past a wetlands lagoon with a tower ahead of us **(NE)**, the route then swinging away from a beach **(57.757N 15.802E, 30M)** to head **NW** into a new valley.

Topping a rise **(57.797N 15.669E)**, the sea comes back into view and we stroll down past a beach before climbing up to pass an old cottage **(57.857N 15.479E)**. We then drop down to the swampy region alongside **Cala sa Torreta (37M)** and our route, now sandy, runs in amongst pine trees and swings right **(57.814N 15.371E, SW)** to emerge facing a boat house. Our route swings left and climbs gently away from the sea. We come up through a gate entrance **(57.861N 15.264E, 41M)** as our track steadily ascends through meadows to a saddle **(45M)**, before descending gently **(NW)**. We walk up past a drinking trough to pass through another gate entrance **(57.871N 14.942E, 50M)**, and now it is a steady ascent through another entrance **(57.898N 14.862E)** and then alongside a stone wall, until we pass through another entrance **(58.016N 14.730E, 58M)** where we catch a glimpse of a modern farm building which indicates that we are finally close to **Torre Blanca** *poblat*. We come up to the farm buildings, turning up to the gate by the breeze block barn. A path on the right of the gate leads around the building to the *poblat* of **Torre Blanca (58.046N 14.612E, 60M)**. The dappled shade provided by overhanging trees adds to the archaeological interest, making this one of Menorca's most attractive historic sites, and just the place to take a break before starting our return to **Es Grau**.

We begin our return **(0M)** by heading south from the farmyard through a gate

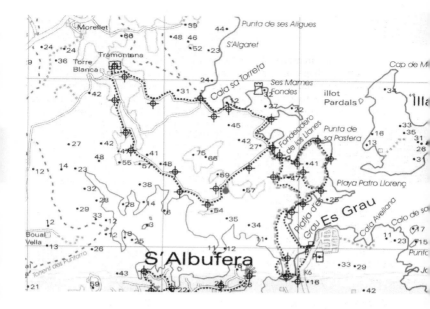

with a cloth tie closure and onto a little-used dirt lane, which brings us to gates on our right latched with a wooden stake **(57.866N 14.692E)**. We go through the gates and over a little rise, and then down through a field entrance to parallel an old donkey trail stuffed with pistacia bushes. We go through another pair of gate posts **(57.698N 14.763E, 10M)** and descend between stone walls before emerging to views across wooded valleys **(57.629N 14.804E)**. Passing a track down to our right **(57.593N 14.789E)**, we then drop down into the next valley with views over **S'Albufera**, to go through another set of gate posts **(57.433N 15.068E)**.

Our path is now little-used and surrounded by an abundance of wild flowers, as we pass a water trough and gate posts **(57.345N 15.155E)**, almost at the waters of the **S'Albufera**. We cross a stream in the next field as our route swings **ESE** to pass through more gate posts **(57.284N 15.308E)** and ascend gently to a well alongside the track **(57.367N 15.424E, 30M)**. Once past the well, we face a steady ascent over a crest **(57.420N 15.476E)** before strolling downhill once more. Rope-latched gates **(57.500N 15.620E)** mark a distinct change from farmed to wild countryside, and we stroll down between slopes reclaimed by nature to meet our outward route **(57.616N 15.789E)**.

Now we retrace our outward route back to the southern end of the beach **(57.536N 15.897E)** to take the inland path. It is a stiff climb up the valley to meet our outward route once more **(57.375N 15.842E, 50M)** amongst the trees. Again we retrace our outward route, and after more than two hours in the countryside, the waterside bars of **Es Grau** prove a powerful magnet to guide us back to base.

24. S'ALBUFERA WALKS

S'Albufera wetlands reserve has three short waymarked walks designed to give views of this protected *Parc Natural* area. The red and green routes both start at the end of the tarmac in the failed urbanization of **Santa Modrono.** To reach the start, drive out of **Es Grau** and take the first turning right, signed to **S'Albufera** reserve. Past the information office on your left, keep straight ahead on the tarmac until it runs out at a parking area marked by a signboard **(56.678N 15.158E)**. The blue route begins from the **Es Grau** car park.

Red Route

We head east **(E)**, climbing over a stone wall by means of its steps and walking up a rough dirt road to a marker post, and on to cross another wall **(56.698N 15.247E)** before coming to a junction. A marker post **(56.721N 15.253E)** directs us straight ahead **(E)** to a signboard illustrating some of the local endemic plants species found in this area **(56.767N 15.372E)**, and on to cross another stone wall with steps. We come outside villa number 164 sitting in splendid isolation **(56.758N 15.423E)**, and then our route swings left to pass a chained entrance **(56.753N 15.456E)** and run down to a saddle and then up to overlook the lagoon. On this final stage, we have *mirador* views over the reserve as our dirt road curves round to finish at a signboard, this time describing some of the birds to be seen in this area **(56.837N 15.629E, 15M)**.

Retrace your steps to return to the parking area.

Green Route

From the car park **(56.678N 15.158E)**, we cross a wall to head **NW** on a wide dirt road which curves left to a Y-junction which is dominated by a large green sign. A marker post sends us along the right road and over a wall by using its steps **(56.749N 15.052E)** to walk between large bushes **(N)**, going gently uphill to a T-junction with an almost blank marker post. We go left **(SW)** and our route narrows to a walking trail before it comes onto another dirt road. *Mirador* views open up as we come to a signboard providing information about some of the bird life of the area **(56.844N 14.910E)**. A marker post directs us up a walking trail, and climbing up through the undergrowth brings us to another marker post **(56.805N 14.921E, 10M)**. Here the green arrow points ahead, but a line of stones across the path shows that we should take the clear path to our right. We push through thorny broom to come onto a broad dirt trail where a marker post shows three (confusing) directions **(56.762N 14.956E)**. Going left, we drop down past an abandoned villa **(56.723N 15.006E)** to the Y-junction with the green signboard. From here we have an easy stroll back along our outward route and to the car park **(15M)**.

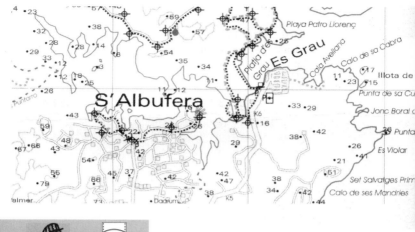

Blue Route

Starting from the **Es Grau** car park **(57.015N 16.106E)**, we head across the beach until we turn left at its northern end onto the **S'Albufera** path, to walk up past a *mirador* sign **(57.206N 15.866E)** on the sandy track. At a plant information board **(57.148N 15.845E)**, a blue waymark points back along our route as we continue on past a sign board **(57.104N 15.846E)** to come to the start of the **S'Albufera**'s impressive walkway over the water **(56.927N 15.902E)**. From here, you have a choice of walking over the water or following the woodland path. The two routes come together again at the end of the walkway **(56.854N 15.935E)**, from where we stroll through the trees to cross a bridge **(56.841N 15.977E)**. All too soon we are leaving the **S'Albufera (56.828N 16.034E)**, to walk back down the road to the **Es Grau** parking area.

S'ALBUFERA WETLANDS

Menorca once boasted many wetland areas but most were drained and the land used for farming or tourist development. The salt water marshes of S'Albufera are safe as the area has been declared a protected Nature Reserve. The main lagoon covers approximately 70 hectares, and provides a wealth of bird-watching opportunities.

Over-wintering birds include the **Cormorant**, **Marsh Harrier**, **Sandwich Tern** and **Alpine Accentor**.

Migrant species include the **Night Heron**, **Little Egret** and **Tawny Pipit**.

Other species to be seen year-round are the **Shearwater**, **Egyptian Vulture**, **Booted Eagle** and the **Sardinian Warbler**.

There are many more; ask for the Govern Balear's leaflet Birds of Minorca (free) in tourist information offices.

25. FORTS ANCIENT AND MODERN

What begins as a country stroll from one of Menorca's important archaeological sites becomes a surprising adventure into some more recent history. Take refreshments with you in order to take time exploring **Lluc al Lari**.

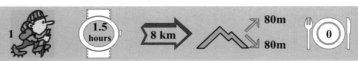

Our starting point is the **Poblat Torre d'en Gaumés** which we reach on the tarmac lane signed off the **Sant Jaume** road, approximately 2.5 kilometres south of **Alaior**. We park in the *poblat*, **(54.248N 07.008E)** and can explore this extensive historic site before heading south on the dirt road which continues on from the tarmac.

It is easy strolling on a gentle descent with views over Menorca's southern plateau, passing the large farmhouse of **Son Vidal** away on our left. Our dirt lane begins to meander **(53.930N 06.711E)**, with few features in this bucolic landscape until we pass a well on our left **(53.744N 06.492E, 15M)** before reaching the entrance gate to **Sa Torre Vella (53.622N 06.394E)**. We pass in front of the house and farmyard with its noisy but not unfriendly dogs, and go through a gate to follow the dirt road **(W)** to drop into a valley lined with caves. A gentle climb **(WSW)** brings us up to pass the old house of **Sant Llorenç** on our right **(53.547N 05.953E, 27M)**, followed shortly by stone seats beneath ancient pines **(53.533N 05.851E, 30M)** before we cross a tarmac lane **(53.518N 05.749E, 32M)**.

Although our ultimate destination is along the lane on our left, we continue on the dirt road **(WSW)** to pass more sets of stone seats beneath ancient pines **(53.514N 05.716E & 53.498N 05.593E)** before coming to a large country mansion **(53.483N 05.494E)**. The mansion was once the quarters for the commander of the coastal fort but has been abandoned and sadly vandalised for some time. Staff quarters and a chapel still stand in its grounds, and the remains of an ornamental garden struggle to maintain some dignity.

We head south from the mansion on an overgrown dirt road which crosses the head of a valley which runs down to the sea on our right. Coming up from the valley, we pass between large gate posts **(53.338N 05.343E)** before the dirt road peters out and buildings come into sight. We pass a circular observation post **(53.301N 05.296E, 45M)** and come into the former **Lluc al Lari** military camp.

Across the open ground, we strike the tarmac lane which comes from **Torre d'en Gaumés**, and our attention is grabbed by the amazing sight of a huge military gun - and not just one gun, as there is a second fifty metres to our right! The underground control rooms for the guns are welded shut, preventing budding militarists from triggering a bombardment, but otherwise this military camp is largely intact. Observation and range-finding positions built into the top of the cliffs offer superb coastal views, these cliff top positions stretching almost a kilometre to the south-east. A dirt road brings us

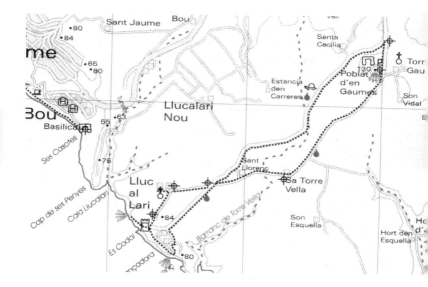

back to the entrance to the base.

For our return **(0M)** we choose the easy stroll on the tarmac lane, usually traffic free though it may become busier as our 'Tour & Trail' Map is the first map to show details of the military camp. Pistacia bushes push in on the road as we pass a well on our right **(53.455N 05.674E)** before coming to the crossroads from our outward route **(53.518N 05.749E, 8M)**. The views ahead are dominated by **Mount Toro** and **Poblat d'en Gaumés** as we stroll past **Sant Llorenç (53.613N 05.896E)** with its large threshing circles.

A gentle downhill section takes us past another well **(54.019N 06.749E, 30M)** and then it is gently uphill between cultivated fields to pass the entrance to **Santa Cecilia (54.313N 06.789E)** with **Poblat d'en Gaumés** looming over us on our right. Unfortunately, there is no short cut to the *poblat* so we stroll up to the junction of the lane **(54.448N 07.104E, 40M)** and then head south to come back to our start point **(54.248N 07.008E)**, 45 minutes from the guns.

POBLAT TORRE D'EN GAUMÉS

In addition to the usual *talaiots* and *taulas*, Torre d'en Gaumés also has a well-preserved *hypostyle* chamber, a low stone-roofed building supported on columns. There are also the remains of a water storage and filtration system carved into the rock, probably added to the original 1400 BC village during Roman times

26. SANT TOMÁS TO COVAS DE COLOMS

This interesting walk takes in a coastal path, a climb on a donkey trail up through a lush valley, and some impressive caves.

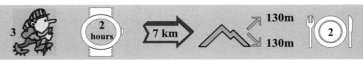

We start by parking behind the bar at the western end of **Sant Tomás** and taking the path around the front of the bar **(55.098N 02.059E, 0M)** to head westwards along the coast. Our narrow path follows the coastline, passing an old pillbox (now used as a boat hut) on our right and islands on our left, to come to the start of the **Platja de Binigaus** beach **(55.188N 01.837E)**. It is reasonably easy walking until our path drops onto the beach **(55.279N 01.650E, 10M)**, where we have to slog across the soft sand towards old pillboxes, then swinging right to come onto a dirt road **(55.354N 01.561E)** by a shanty; actually a jovial Spanish pensioner's sculpture workshop.

Now it is easy walking along the dirt road **(N)** through the shallow valley until we pass through a gate **(55.486N 01.565E, 20M)** where a sign directs us onto a walking trail. Over a wall on a stepping stone, our narrow trail curves round from east to north as we cross small fields before crossing another wall **(55.550N 01.735E)**. Now the trail cuts across the tree-covered, sloping valley side **(N)** where there is little sign of human habitation except for the squared-off stones on the left side of the path **(55.629N 01.748E)**. Pruners would be useful as bushes push in on our path - beware of occasional thorns - until we zigzag up through a wall to come onto a cobbled donkey trail **(55.768N 01.828E)** and a junction.

The right hand path leads across the valley floor to **Cova des Coloms** (not signed), one of the huge caves for which this valley is famous. Back at the junction, we continue on the main path in a gentle ascent, crossing another wall **(55.875N 02.026E, 50M)**, with the landscape becoming gentler as we approach the valley's upper reaches. At another wall **(55.880N 02.268E)**, a small path goes right to more caves while we continue **(N)** on the main path, keeping left when the path forks.

At the next junction **(55.971N 02.333E)** we go left, ascending the valley wall, and then the trail levels out and we come to a signed junction; '5 minutes to the caves' **(56.054N 02.360E, 60M)**. We take the steep path down to cross the valley floor for a steady climb up through zigzags to the cave entrance **(56.036N 02.390E, 65M)**. Through a defile, we come into the cathedral-sized cave. Despite its dimensions, the cave is well lit at floor level, while bats squeak high up on the dark, cavernous roof.

Back at the junction **(0M)** on the west side of the valley, we continue inland **(N)** on the path, which becomes boulder-laid and climbs steadily to pass through a wall **(56.113N 02.366E)**. Steady climbing brings us up and out of the valley and onto a plateau where we stroll over to a signboard beside a dirt

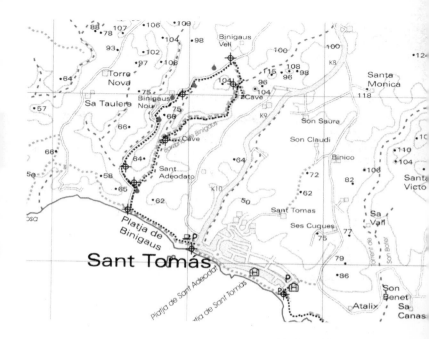

road **(56.201N 02.331E, 10M)**. Our route is left **(SW)**, though going right would take you to **Es Migjorn Gran** in about 30-40 minutes of walking.

After the climb up and out of the valley, our return is an easy stroll **(SW)** down past a well **(56.134N 02.219E)** and then through a gated entrance **(56.099N 02.106E, 15M)** as views open up over the valley to our right. A gentle uphill section takes us past another well **(56.055N 02.020E)** before strolling down to pass through the gates of **Binigaus Nou (55.974N 01.903E)**. Passing in front of the house, we go through another set of gates, and our trail starts to drop down into the valley past another well **(55.857N 01.758E, 25M)**. Our route zigzags down to the valley floor and heads seawards **(SW)**, curving south for us to pass through a gated entrance, and then along to join our outward route by the signboard **(55.486N 01.565E, 38M)**. From here, we retrace our outward route to arrive back on the bar terrace **(55.098N 02.059E, 60M)**.

27. SANT TOMÁS - SON BOU

This popular route between **Sant Tomás** and **Son Bou** looks easy on a map, but much of the walk is on soft sand, making it much tougher than it looks. Also, it is best to avoid windy days when the blowing sand can make the dunes a survival exercise.

3 | 2 hours | 8 km | 40m / 40m | 2

We start out from below **Hotel Victoria**, by the signboard, 'Platja d'Atalitx 25M, Platja Son Bou 1H' **(54.829N 02.684E, 0M)** to climb up from the beach **(SE)** past a cave and onto **Punta Negra**. This rocky area **(54.761N 02.741E)** has no formal paths, so we keep heading **SSE** to come across the headland. Ahead, **Son Bou** comes into view **(54.699N 02.753E)** while closer to hand, pimples of rock puncture the azure sea along the rugged coastline. Inland meadows ablaze with wild flowers run up to the edge of pine woods as we come onto a more defined coastal path **(SE)**. We begin to pass tiny bays on our right **(54.616N 03.107E, 12M)** with the **Atalitx** country estate inland of us, as we stroll along to a bridge **(54.531N 03.247E, 15M)** over the **Torrent Son Boter** which runs into its impressive bay. Across the bridge, the idyllic little beach of **Platges d'Atalitx** is on our right, as we walk along to pass through a gate **(54.526N 03.374E)** and drop down to the start of **Platges de Son Bou**.

We are now into serious beach and sand dune territory, with our destination of **San Bou** still over two kilometres away. Our choice is between the soft sand beach, the slightly firmer damp sand along the sea's edge, or the low, grassy dunes. Whichever option we choose, it is still a slog - far tougher than it appears on a map. On our left, the lagoon and wetlands of **Sant Jaume**, edged with reeds and bamboo thickets, form a boundary to the dunes. We head **SE** past an island, sculpted by erosion into the image of a cruising ship **(approx. 54.412N 03.695E, 28M)**. Gradually, the 'cozzie optional' nature of the beach gives way to family groups as we come down to the lagoon's outlet into the sea **(54.144N 04.200E)** which flows only as a narrow stream except after heavy rain.

Across the outlet, we come onto a fully commercial beach with opportunities for refreshments and beach or sea activities. We can leave the beach on a sand road **(54.058N 04.326E, 45M)** though our logical route is to continue past the **Milanos** and **Pinguinos** hotels **(53.931N 04.598E, 50M)** to the walled-in *basilica*, the remains of an early Christian church at the end of the beach **(53.837N 04.776E, 55M)**. Don't expect too many distractions in the pocket resort of **Son Bou** before your return to **Sant Tomás** - and nearly three kilometres of soft sand before reaching the solid ground after **Platges d'Atalitx**!

28. CIUTADELLA TOWN WALK

Ciutadella's long and sometimes turbulent history is still preserved in its noble buildings and ancient palaces. Its central area around the Cathedral has a cosmopolitan, sophisticated atmosphere. It is easy to see why it was once the island's capital, and was the most desirable place to live on Menorca.

| 1 | 1.5 hours | 4-5 km | 20m / 20m | 4 |

If you arrive by bus from the beach resorts south of the city, the ride terminates at **Plaça Esplanada**. Buses from other areas finish at the bus station on **Carrer Barcelona**. Car drivers will find parking tricky although there is a chance of spaces at **Plaça d'es Born**; otherwise, be prepared to park on the outskirts of the town.

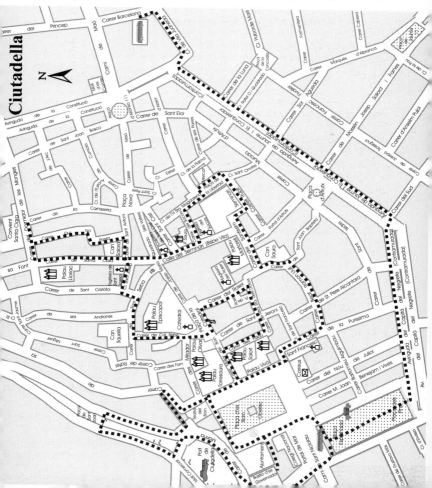

The walk proper begins at **Plaça Esplanada**, so those arriving at the bus station or parking on the edge of town need to make their way to this point. To avoid getting lost, follow the broad **Avingudas** which are built on the lines of the old city walls. Heading west will soon bring you to **Plaça Esplanda**.

We cross the road with the bus stops on it on the north of the square and bear right into **Plaça d'es Born** marked by its towering **Obelisk** commemorating those who lost their lives in the Turkish invasion of 1558 which flattened most of the town. Occupying the north-west corner of the square is the **Ajuntament** with its stone arches and stately palms. Step inside to examine the Gothic reception areas and memorabilia including portraits of past dignitaries. This is a 'working' town hall so you can go inside during office hours and from 18.00 to 20.00 hours on weekdays. Turning right as we leave the town hall, we take the steps leading up to the viewpoint of **Bastió d'es Governador** (17th century) tower to overlook the harbour.

Back in **Plaça d'es Born**, we cross to its east side, dominated by **Palau Torresaura** with the family coat-of-arms carved over its main archway. On its right stands **Palau Salort** on the corner of **Carrer Major del Born**, open for viewing in summer (10.00-14.00). We continue clockwise round the square passing **Palau Vivó** to face one of the few churches to survive the Turkish destruction, the Gothic **Església de Sant Francesc**, with baroque additions. We walk along **Carrer de la Purissima** by the side of the church and take the second left, **Carrer de Beat Ramon Llull**, following it to its T-junction with **Carrer de Sant Joan Baptista**. We turn left onto the street, and then first right into **Carrer del Santissim**.

We are entering one of the interesting shopping streets of this old central area; for example, the antique and furniture restoration shop on the right is housed in the elegant **Can Saura** (17th century), and we pass leather, silk and craft shops as well as **Palau Martorell**, the austere residence of the Marques de Albranca, on our left towards the top of the street. Keeping on this street as it angles around the **Seminari** which houses the **Diocesan Museum**, brings us onto **Castell Rupit** and on into **Plaça de la Libertad**. We can take a few minutes to look around the fruit, vegetable and fish market (**Mercat**) in the square.

Leaving the square on the **Carrer de l'Hospital de Santa Magdalena** at its north-west corner, we then take the first left (**Carrer del Socors**) which leads us to **Calle del Seminari**, a shopper's paradise of small specialist shops. On the corner as we enter the street stands **Església del Socors** on the left, and a bank occupies what was **Palau Saura** on the right. We go right along the street, passing the little baroque chapel of **Capella de Sant Crist** (1667) with its octagonal dome, on our right.

We carry on ahead to meet and cross **Carrer de Josep Maria Quadrado** to the street opposite which angles slightly right, **Carrer de Santa Clara**. We walk along past **Església de Sant Josep** on the left and **Can Salord** on the right before passing the austere lines of **Palau Lloriac** on the left. We take the next right onto **Carrer del Dormidor de les Monges** and walk along to take a look at **Convent Santa Clara** on the north side of the road, its original buildings dating back to 1287 but rebuilt after the Turkish invasion, and restored again in the twentieth century.

We double back for a few metres to go left down **Carrer Qui No Passa** to its T-junction with **Carrer de Sant Antoni** where we turn right around the corner of **Can Salord** and walk the few metres to meet **Carrer de Santa Clara**. We cross straight over and take the short street almost opposite, **Carrer Sant Josep** with the church on its corner. A left at the next junction brings us to **Carrer de Sant Sebastiá.**

Turning right, we walk west along **Carrer de Sant Sebastiá** and take the next turning left onto **Carrer de Cal Bisbe**. The building on our left is the **Palau Episcopal**, the Bishop's residence which shares a site with the **Catedral** itself, dedicated to St. Mary. A mosque once stood here, and although a Christian church occupied this area from 1362, it was destroyed by the Turks in 1558 and gradually rebuilt. The newest addition to the building is the west wing, on the corner as we enter **Plaça de la Catedral** with the **Tourist Information Office** opposite. On the other side of this corner stands **Palau Olivar**, yet another grand home owned by one of the elite families, the Olives.

We leave the square on **Carrer de Roser** opposite the older south door of the **Catedral**. This street is the location of more small specialist shops, and also the eye-catchingly ornate baroque **Església del Roser** about half way along it on the left, now used as an exhibition venue. At the end of the street we turn right onto **Carrer de Notra Senora dels Dolors**, keeping on it as it bends right and becomes **Carrer des Palau** before it meets the T-junction with **Carrer Major del Born** with the **Palau Torresaura** facing us. We go left here and are now back in **Plaça des Born**.

Heading right to the north side of the square, we pass the **Teatro del Born** theatre as we enter **Carrer de sa Muradeta**, looking out for steps down to the harbour on our left after the street angles left and right. After strolling around the harbour area, we find another flight of steps off the **Carrer de Marina** behind the town hall (**Ajuntament**) which take us back up to street level onto **Camí de Sant Nicolau** which leads us back to our starting point in **Plaça Esplanada**.

CIUTADELLA - More to see

Do ask in the tourist information office, opposite the Cathedral, for up to date details of places to visit and opening times. The rich and colourful history of this town provides plenty of interest.

One place not to be missed if you want to get a feel for Ciutadella's past, as well as the history of Menorca from prehistoric times, is the Museu Municipal. It is housed in the fortress of Bastió de sa Font (in the north-west of the town) which has had a variety of uses until its renovation as the city's museum in 1995.

There are museums of art and museums of ecclesiastical interest, and plenty to fascinate those interested in architecture - or why not climb the 73 steps to the top of the windmill of Molí des Comte (on the eastern edge of the town near Plaça d'Alfonso) for panoramic views of the town.

29. SANTA AGUEDA

To reach the start, we turn off the **Ciutadella - Ferreries** road (C-721) onto the **Camí d'es Alocs** road, and drive north until we come to the modernist but abandoned school house by the gated entrance to **Santa Ceclia**. There is space for four or five cars to park, but take care not to block the road or entrance.

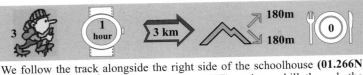

3   1 hour   3 km   180m / 180m   0

We follow the track alongside the right side of the schoolhouse (**01.266N 00.147E**), going uphill through the metal gates. Water erosion has removed the stone surface on this lower part of the route, leading to muddiness in wet weather, but in a couple of minutes we come onto the remains of boulder-laid sections as we climb up between trees (**NE**). Passing through a stone wall (**01.391N 00.280E, 5M**), we continue upwards through denser trees, and our route swings **ENE** (**01.426N 00.340E, 8M**) as we continue relentlessly upwards. Gradually our route swings back towards the north to come alongside an old stone wall (**01.480N 00.446E, 12M**) for us to come onto the original stone-laid surface of the path.

The path ahead appears to be blocked off, though a dirt path swings right (**E**) before climbing through a hairpin bend (**01.487N 00.472E**) to pass a field entrance on our right and come through a gate and back onto the old stone-laid trail (**01.511N 00.445E, 17M**); the adventurous can cut off this dirt path section by continuing on the stone-laid path and scrambling up the boulders and onto the path's continuation by the gate.

As we climb steadily alongside the wall (**N**), views across the northern landscapes open up, and we come to a shed on our right (**01.628N 00.478E, 22M**) and the more surprising sight of a 1930's car rusting away beside our trail. Now we are climbing seriously (**N**) to pass onto a section of zigzags (**01.696N 00.416E, 01.682N 00.483E, 01.711N 00.463E**). The bends make good rest points from which to admire what remains of the castle walls before we tackle the final slopes (**01.686N 00.523E**) up to the abandoned farm buildings which occupy this historic site (**01.701N 00.536E, 30M**). Although virtually nothing remains of the old castle, from the plateau on the peak we enjoy spectacular views before returning by the same route down to our car.

30. GALDANA GORGE

This is an easy walk along the spectacular **Galdana** gorge. Stunning scenery, flora and bird life make this route a must for everyone. Virtually flat, you only need to cross a small wall on stepping stones, so lack of fitness is no excuse!

We start at the roundabout **(56.480N 57.633E)** at the end of the bridge and follow the pavement east and north past the bars and shops until we pass **Galdana Palms** and come onto a dirt road **(56.708N 57.802E, 10M)** which takes us up to a pair of metal gates **(56.754N 57.751E, 12M)**. Stepping stones alongside the gates allow us pedestrian access. You might find bamboo staves have been left here for the use of walkers.

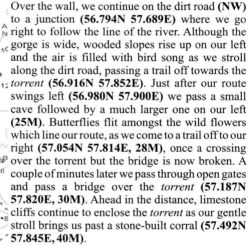

Over the wall, we continue on the dirt road **(NW)** to a junction **(56.794N 57.689E)** where we go right to follow the line of the river. Although the gorge is wide, wooded slopes rise up on our left and the air is filled with bird song as we stroll along the dirt road, passing a trail off towards the *torrent* **(56.916N 57.852E)**. Just after our route swings left **(56.980N 57.900E)** we pass a small cave followed by a much larger one on our left **(25M)**. Butterflies flit amongst the wild flowers which line our route, as we come to a trail off to our right **(57.054N 57.814E, 28M)**, once a crossing over the torrent but the bridge is now broken. A couple of minutes later we pass through open gates and pass a bridge over the *torrent* **(57.187N 57.820E, 30M)**. Ahead in the distance, limestone cliffs continue to enclose the *torrent* as our gentle stroll brings us past a stone-built corral **(57.492N 57.845E, 40M)**.

Now the river bed is choked with bamboo thickets, making for a closed-in feel until we swing left **(NW)** and the gorge opens up again below superb limestone cliffs **(57.625N 57.861E, 43M)**. Across the open area, we come to a cultivated field, fenced with reinforcing mesh **(57.661N 57.780E)** and our broad trail narrows to a single file track. We continue on with bushes pushing in on the route, until we meet the limit of navigation **(57.733N 57.916E, 48M)**.

We return by retracing our steps through this natural wonderland, remembering to leave the bamboo staves at the wall for other walkers, finally seeking refreshment in the resort while savouring the memories of this spectacular but easy experience of Menorca.

31. CALA GALDANA TO CALA MACARELLA

Starting from the roundabout in the centre of **Serpentona**, we walk alongside the river **(W & SW)** until the road swings sharp right to the entrance of **Hotel Audax (56.397N 57.492E, 5M)**. Here we have two routes to choose from; short and energetic, or longer but on better paths.

Short and Energetic Route

From the corner we go up the stairs, and where the crowds go left over the bridge, we keep straight on. The broad path soon narrows as it climbs amongst the pines, and we look down on the clear waters of the inlet. The rule is 'onwards and upwards' **(SW & W)** as we duck under a fallen tree and then climb up through a zigzag **(56.323N 57.422E)**. Steady climbing brings us up to a junction **(56.336N 57.309E, 12M)** where we come onto a broad trail by a fire warning sign.

Longer Scenic Route

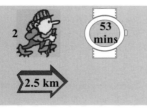

Continue on the road past **Hotel Audax**, and when the road turns right again, we fork left onto a road which climbs north-west **(NW)**. We pass a steep flight of stairs on our right **(56.453N 57.375E)**, our **Ciutadella** route, before the road narrows down to a track which continues to climb steeply **(NW)**. Fifteen minutes from our start **(15M)** our track meets two dirt roads at **Car Wreck Junction (56.569N 57.202E)** where we turn left **(S)** for an easy stroll through the woods. Passing a loop of the dirt road on our left **(56.406N 57.293E)** and **(56.343N 57.331E)**, we come to the fire warning sign junction **(56.336N 57.309E, 23M)** to meet our 'Short and Energetic' route option.

From the junction **(0M)** we head west **(W)** on the broad, gladioli-lined trail, passing a walking trail off to our left **(56.325N 57.151E).** Then our route swings south-west **(SW)** and the trail splits **(56.292N 57.016E)**, left for pushchairs, coming together again after a small rock outcrop. Our wide trail meanders along with very gentle gradients, the direction swinging between south-west and north-west **(SW** to **NW)** until we come to the edge of a deep valley which runs down to **Cala Macarella (56.345N 56.511E)**. We go down into a shallow valley where the broad trail splits into two paths **(56.371N 56.460E)**.

On our left, a path runs out a few metres to a viewing point while we start down the main path on a steep, almost staired rock descent. Take care on this descent which passes two minor trails coming in from our right, dropping down under the trees to the gate onto the beach at **Cala Macarella 56.376N 56.337E, 30M)**; watch out for the step down from the gate! Total time for 'Short and Energetic' route **(42M)** and for 'Longer Scenic' route, **(53M)**.

On our right is the welcoming sight of the **Bar Suzy** (open from approximately 11.00 onwards in season) shaded by trees in contrast to the gleaming white sand of the bay.

BEACHES, BEACHES

If you love beaches then Menorca is your island. The two *calas* linked by this walk are both beautiful, Cala Galdana offering pine-edged white sand and hotels, restaurants and water sports while Cala Macarella offers refreshments and a sheltered cove shaded by pines.

If these serve only to whet your appetite, there are plenty more to choose from, although the romantic claim that there are 365 beaches is rather optimistic; the figure is around 120, and some can be reached only on foot or by sea.

This long, mostly coastal route takes in stunning views, beaches and bays and a sense of history. Do take plenty of water, as the major part of the walk is without refreshment stops.

4 · **3¾ hours** · **15 km** · 230m / 230m · **2**

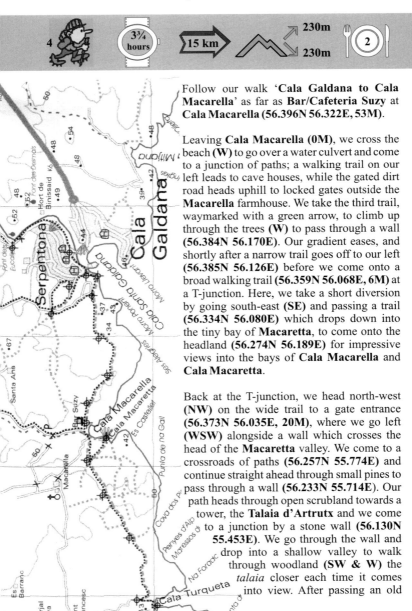

Follow our walk 'Cala Galdana to Cala Macarella' as far as Bar/Cafeteria Suzy at Cala Macarella (56.396N 56.322E, 53M).

Leaving **Cala Macarella (0M)**, we cross the beach **(W)** to go over a water culvert and come to a junction of paths; a walking trail on our left leads to cave houses, while the gated dirt road heads uphill to locked gates outside the **Macarella** farmhouse. We take the third trail, waymarked with a green arrow, to climb up through the trees **(W)** to pass through a wall **(56.384N 56.170E)**. Our gradient eases, and shortly after a narrow trail goes off to our left **(56.385N 56.126E)** before we come onto a broad walking trail **(56.359N 56.068E, 6M)** at a T-junction. Here, we take a short diversion by going south-east **(SE)** and passing a trail **(56.334N 56.080E)** which drops down into the tiny bay of **Macaretta**, to come onto the headland **(56.274N 56.189E)** for impressive views into the bays of **Cala Macarella** and **Cala Macaretta**.

Back at the T-junction, we head north-west **(NW)** on the wide trail to a gate entrance **(56.373N 56.035E, 20M)**, where we go left **(WSW)** alongside a wall which crosses the head of the **Macaretta** valley. We come to a crossroads of paths **(56.257N 55.774E)** and continue straight ahead through small pines to pass through a wall **(56.233N 55.714E)**. Our path heads through open scrubland towards a tower, the **Talaia d'Artrutx** and we come to a junction by a stone wall **(56.130N 55.453E)**. We go through the wall and drop into a shallow valley to walk through woodland **(SW & W)** the *talaia* closer each time it comes into view. After passing an old

stone-cutting area on our left, we swing into the **Turqueta** valley (**56.061N 54.957E, 50M**) to emerge by the water wheel at the seaward end of the parking area (pay parking).

From **Turqueta** beach, we head up a narrow path marked with a red arrow (**56.004N 54.912E**) to pass through a small stone wall and onto a rocky path which takes us above a second inlet and a boathouse. Once across a gully, we come onto a broad track which heads inland, passing a path off to our left but taking the next trail left and south (**S**) (**55.999N 54.853E**) to climb away from **Cala Turqueta**. We soon reach another junction (**55.954N 54.865E, 60M**) where we go right (**SW**) and uphill towards the **Talaia d'Artutx**, occasionally in view. Across a cleared firebreak area (**55.890N 54.763E**), our trail climbs towards the tower and we come up to the old abandoned house of **Sa Cuesta** at the base of the tower (**55.840N 54.681E, 70M**).

After enjoying the views over our onward route, we take a little-used dirt road to head towards (**NNW**) the impressive mansion of **Malfaui**. Through a stone wall, and just as we think that the route must go to **Malfaui**, we come to a gate alongside the main dirt road (**56.046N 54.472E, 80M**). Climbing stones take us over the wall and onto the broad dirt road (cars, 700ptas each) which runs through a stone wall (**55.864N 54.301E**) and past a faint junction (**55.777N 54.207E**) to come onto a walking trail (**55.739N 54.202E**) where we overlook **Cala d'es Talaier**. We head south-west (**SW**) between gateposts (**55.673N 54.167E, 82M**), and keep right at a junction (**55.651N 54.144E**) to pass a bunker on our left. There are various tracks amongst the dunes and scrub though we keep **WNW** between the beach and the wetlands to come to old gun positions which overlook the beach (**55.752N 53.792E, 100M**).

Many writers praise this cozzie-optional bay of **Son Saurer** for its lack of development, but in our opinion it would be much improved by the addition of one small development - a *tipico* beach bar!

After enjoying the near-idyllic **Son Saurer** bay, we head off towards **Cala'n Bosch (0M)**. At the western end of the beach (**55.738N 53.535E**) we meet a dirt road and take the walking trail (**WSW**), to pass another trail on our right before going through a gate in a stone wall (**55.695N 53.512E**). We keep straight ahead when the trail splits (**8M**) and go past another path on our right, before passing another gun position overlooking the bay (**55.603N 53.454E**). Keeping to the main path, we curve round (**W**) to overlook the azure waters of the inlet beside **Punta Barraqueta** (**55.506N 53.293E, 14M**).

We cross the head of the inlet to keep west over rocky, open ground to another gun position (**55.512N 53.116E, 20M**) at a junction, where we go left through an old wall. Following the trail, we cross the head of an inlet (**55.461N 53.058E**) to keep west (**W**) above the cliffs on the faint trail. We pass between caves dug either side of the trail (**55.423N 55.565E, 33M**) before meeting a steel gate (**55.441N 52.462E, 35M**).

Once through the gate, we follow the track which widens to a dirt road (**55.558N 52.197E, 44M**) as we pass through a wall and a track off to our left. We come to a machine gun post at a gate entrance (**55.527N 51.976E**) where we take a trail to our left (**S**). We go south and then turn right (**W**) at a junction (**55.426N 51.986E**) to walk alongside a recently built stone wall.

After passing through a gate (**55.422N 51.720E, 57M**), we get our first views of **Cala'n Bosch** as we pass a private entry to **Son Parets Nou** on our right and a hut on our left, followed by a stone-built gun emplacement (**55.473N 51.401E, 64M**).

We come level with the development of **Son Xoriguer** inland of us as the broad trail curves **WNW** and we walk alongside the bay of **Son Xoriguer**. The final section into **Cala'n Bosch** is easy to follow, as we take the path around **Platja Son Xoriguer** and out onto **Punta Guarda** which then heads north-west (**NW**) past **Cala'n Bosch** bay and to the bus stop opposite the hotel. However, after 75 minutes walking from **Son Saurer**, the sight of welcoming bars to the north of us (**55.591N 50.774E**) is too much of a temptation. We take a small path across to the **King Kong** and **Miramar** bars after well over three hours of non-stop walking from our start at **Cala Galdana** (**228M** or 3 hours 48 minutes), to substantially increase the island's beverage sales before tackling the final short stage to the bus stop.

33. CALA GALDANA - CIUTADELLA

Breakfast in **Cala Galdana** and lunch in **Ciutadella**, and all without using a car or bus. While this is a long walk, it is an easy stroll through bucolic countryside on quiet country lanes, once we have climbed up onto the plateau. Choose between two routes to reach **Santa Galdana**, where the routes join to go on to **Ciutadella**.

3 | **4 hours** | **16 km** | 150m / 150m | **4** (in Ciutadella)

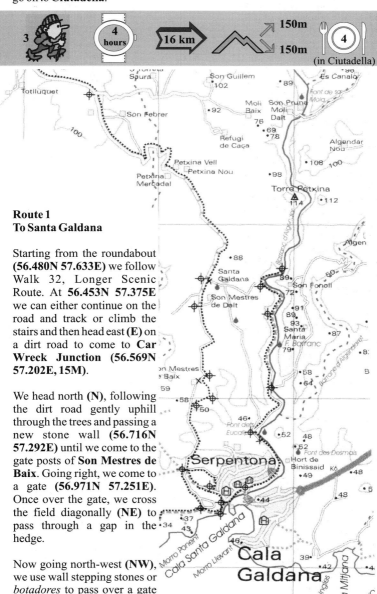

Route 1
To Santa Galdana

Starting from the roundabout **(56.480N 57.633E)** we follow Walk 32, Longer Scenic Route. At **56.453N 57.375E** we can either continue on the road and track or climb the stairs and then head east **(E)** on a dirt road to come to **Car Wreck Junction (56.569N 57.202E, 15M)**.

We head north **(N)**, following the dirt road gently uphill through the trees and passing a new stone wall **(56.716N 57.292E)** until we come to the gate posts of **Son Mestres de Baix**. Going right, we come to a gate **(56.971N 57.251E)**. Once over the gate, we cross the field diagonally **(NE)** to pass through a gap in the hedge.

Now going north-west **(NW)**, we use wall stepping stones or *botadores* to pass over a gate

(57.057N 57.348E). A dirt lane takes us behind **Son Mestres de Baix** and then heads inland **(N)** to swing right by a large pine and then left, before the lane becomes tarmac surfaced **(57.526N 57.301E)** for us to stroll along to the entrance gates of **Santa Galdana (57.678N 57.348E, 45M)**.

Route 2 to Santa Galdana

Starting from the roundabout, follow Walk 30 to the junction of dirt roads **(56.794N 57.689E, 15M)**. Taking the uphill dirt road, we climb through the mature pines in a steady ascent. The gradient eases and we pass between gate posts, gradually leaving the trees behind as we come onto the plateau farmlands. We pass gate entrances to the fields and then walk in front of the **Santa Galdana** farmhouse with its well and peacocks, climbing over the entrance gates and onto a tarmac lane **(57.678N 57.348E, 40M)**.

Continuation for both Route 1&2

We head along the narrow lane **(NNE)**, an easy stroll through the quiet countryside **(NNE** and then **NNW)** as the lane climbs gently up to the farmhouses of **Torre Petxina**, **Petxina Vell**, **Petxina Nou** and **Petxina Mercadal (58.335N 57.086E, 60M)**. Once past the farmhouses, the lane widens to a country road and leads us down across a valley, before climbing up past the entrance to **Son Febrer (58.408N 56.842E)**. We pass a second entrance to **Son Febrer (58.643N 56.561E)** before coming to the **S'Torreta** junction **(58.797N 56.520E, 80M)**.

Continuing on **(NW)**, we pass the entrances to **Totlluc** and **Totlluquet** before we come to **Torre Trencada (59.228N 55.497E, 110M)**, just one of Menorca's sites of historic importance. We suggest that you treat this route as a long stroll, rather than a race - take time out to explore the prehistoric sites along the way.

Back on the lane, now accompanied by some hire car traffic, we stroll along **(NE)**, passing **Son Formatge** on our left, before arriving at a signed road junction

(59.781N 54.366E, 140M). An easy stroll takes us gently down to **Es Tudons** farm entrance on our left **(00.063N 53.508E, 160M)**, and on our right is the unsigned track to **Es Tudons** prehistoric site. Five minutes along this track, we come to Menorca's best known *naveta* **(00.255N 53.563E)**.

We return to the tarmac road **(175M)** and are now heading directly for **Ciutadella (WNW)**, to pass through an area of impressive sheer sided quarries **(00.272N 52.364E, 200M)** on each side of the narrow road. Once past the main quarries, houses and other buildings are dotted along the road as we continue along, passing a sports stadium before coming to the southern ring road of **Ciutadella (220M)**. Following the main streets brings us into the heart of the historic city centre around the cathedral, offering us a wide choice of *tipicos* for refreshments **(230M)**.

ES TUDONS

Many of Menorca's prehistoric sites still lay hidden in uncultivated fields, as was Es Tudons until the late 1950s. Since then, this area and in particular its *naveta* have been painstakingly restored.

This example has two floors. The upper storey was used to place the bodies of the dead, and the ground floor (the ossuary) for storing their bones. Excavations showed that more than 100 individuals had been interred here, including some still wearing items of jewellery.

34. CALA MACARELLA TO CIUTADELLA

This is another long country stroll across the western plateau of Menorca to **Ciutadella**. If you plan to follow Walk 32, Cala Galdana to Cala Macarella in order to reach our starting point, you will need to add an additional 45 minutes, 2.5 kilometres and 50 metres of ascents and descents to this walk.

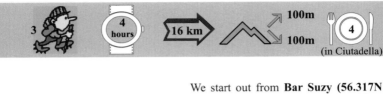

3 | 4 hours | 16 km | 100m / 100m | 4 (in Ciutadella)

We start out from **Bar Suzy (56.317N 56.337E)** in **Cala Macarella**, seldom open, unfortunately, before 11.00. We follow the dirt road heading inland, going past the vehicle barrier and the meadow car parking area **(56.595N 56.216E)**. Past an old water wheel **(56.682N 56.296E)** opposite a spring and where the valley narrows, our route climbs between wooded slopes. Climbing steadily through the trees, we pass the dirt road entrance to **Santa Ana (56.968N 56.603E, 18M)** before crossing the stream bed (muddy in wet weather) to climb steeply up from the valley.

As we climb out of the trees our road changes to rough stone as we stroll past walled meadows, passing **Torralba** farmhouse **(57.551N 56.236E, 40M)** where litters of squeaky piglets are often seen running about.

After a few metres, the lane's surface becomes tarmacked **(57.632N 56.163E)** for easy walking, along to **Torralbet** farmhouse **(57.834N 55.969E)**, where the lane widens into a country road. Now it is easy strolling through the meadow landscape **(NW)**, passing the dirt road leading to **Bellaventura** on our right **(58.228N 54.978E)** to reach the road junction by **Morvedra Vei (58.537N 54.396E, 80M)**, where we decide on one of two onward routes.

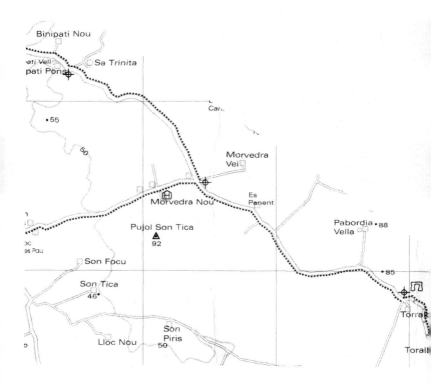

Route 1

The most direct route from the road junction at **Morvedra Vei** continues straight ahead **(NW)** to pass **Sa Trinita** and **Binipati Pons (59.199N 53,447E, 100M)**. Easy walking takes us on **(NW)** until the road swings west **(W)** at **Rafal Nou (59.940N 52.211E, 130M)** to head directly towards **Ciutadella**.

As we approach the city, the country road swings right at a junction **(59.937N 51.366E, 140M)**. We follow this road north **(N)** which brings us up to join the **Ciutadella** ring road near the cemetery, from where we follow the main streets into the city's historic centre **(155M)**.

Route 2

At the road junction by **Morvedra Vei**, we go left **(W)** on the narrower lane and stroll past the exclusive **Morvedra Nou Hotel Rural (58.498N 54.144E)** and occasional houses, to reach the eastern entrance of **Sant Joan de Mises (58.186N 52.970E, 115M)**. This *ermita* dates from 1287 and celebrates St. John the Baptist's birthday on June 24, with skilled displays of horsemanship.

From the junction at **Sant Joan de Mises** we follow the road **(NNW)** towards **Ciutadella**, passing an old cross **(58.588N 52.560E)** before coming to a junction **(58.786N 52.110E, 135M)** signed left to **Platges Saura**, and back along the way we have come to **Platja Macarella**. Following the main road

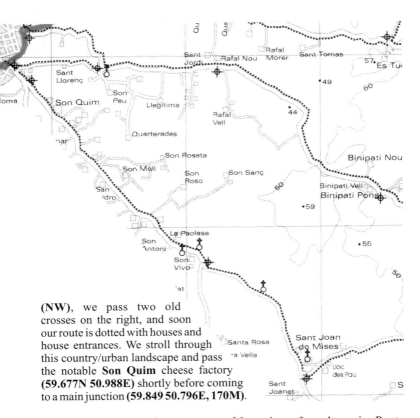

(NW), we pass two old crosses on the right, and soon our route is dotted with houses and house entrances. We stroll through this country/urban landscape and pass the notable **Son Quim** cheese factory **(59.677N 50.988E)** shortly before coming to a main junction **(59.849 50.796E, 170M)**.

Following the main road, we meet one of the options of our alternative Route 1 coming along a lane from our right, just before meeting the **Ciutadella** ring road at a roundabout **(59.953N 50.664E)**. Across the roundabout, the streets leads us towards the historic heart of the city **(184M)**.

ajuntament	town hall
apartamento	apartment
avinguda	avenue
baix	low
barranco	ravine
basilica	early Christian Romanesque church
bastió	stronghold
bini	sons
botadores	stepping stones built into a wall
cala	cove or creek
caló	little cove
camí	old road
camino	donkey trail
camino real	major donkey trail, old 'royal' trail
carrer	street
carretera	road
casa	house
castell	castle
costa	coast
dalt	high
ermita	small church or chapel
església	church
hostal	hostel, lodgings
hypostyle chamber	prehistoric chamber, partly underground
hypostyle	with stone roof supported on pillars
illa	island
jutjat	lawcourts
lluc	farmhouse
mar	sea
mercat	market
mirador	viewing point
moll	quay, harbour
museu	museum
naveta	prehistoric boat-shaped building
nou	new
palau	palace
parc	park
passeig	pedestrian way
plaça	town square
platja	beach
playa	beach
poblat	prehistoric village
pont	bridge
port	port
pou	well, spring
san, sant	saint
son	farmhouse
talaiot	prehistoric cone-shaped stone mound
taula	prehistoric T-shaped stone monument
teatro	theatre
tipico	local bar or restaurant
torrent	stream
vell	old

INDEX OF PLACE NAMES